The Devil Hates a Coward

A Collection of Stories

Peter Hamilton

Copyright © 2014 by Peter Hamilton
First Edition

Without limiting the rights under copyright reserved above, no part of this publication may be reproduced, stored in or introduced into a retrieval system, or transmitted, in any form or by any means (electronic, mechanical, photocopying, recording, or otherwise), without the prior written permission of both the copyright owner and the publisher of this book.

The contents and characters in this book are fictional. Any resemblance to actual persons or happenings is coincidental.

ISBN-10: 1497459702
ISBN-13: 978-1497459700
Printed in the United States of America
ALL RIGHTS RESERVED

With great respect to Riley and Shelby, my adult children, who are one pair that can beat a royal flush on any table, all night long.

To other writers:
  It is all like life: progress not perfection. I claim writing progress, not writing perfection.

Contents

Houdini ~7

Sky Diving ~53

The Adja N'Gor Torch Light ~81

You Do Not Think About Your Kaleidoscope ~89

Into The Flame ~145

Bufflehead ~155

Heart Knots ~243

Houdini

Stewart drove through the late-afternoon flurries—the playful type that drop carelessly as if risk-loving adolescent acrobats, catching a draft swaying upward, trying to ascend to a higher place, another swing, but instead slip, tumble, and plunge—taunting his windshield.

The earlier, mid-morning snow had attempted those falling stunts also, but had matured with heaviness and descended into plump, settled drifts; willful and unmoved, they draped all things with a somber blanket. Stewart maneuvered around what they'd hidden, warily calculating them for snags or ditches. Tree stumps. The potential of a roadside hazard brought forth predictions of a wedged car, the futile whirl of wheels, the arrival of a condescending beer-breath tow-truck operator, the exchange of Stewart's precious cash machine money for the driver's oil-crumpled smaller bills, the misconstrued over-the-shoulder second-look from a clearly hetero-husky man, all of which would leave Stewart with a soul-deep despair that would not thaw until warmed by a sympathetic lover.

Stewart stared hard through the windshield, mindful of a stuck vehicle and the vision of a demeaning truck driver, and focused his attention onto the deserted road ahead. The wipers pulsed a two-four tempo; left-right, left-right. They made prismatic arcs as they streaked through the sparkled washer fluid.

The unplowed road to Lake Chatumn wasn't a pleasant task at the end of a two-hour, blizzard-driven challenge. Stewart had let go of some the drive's stress, yet he still clutched the wheel steadily with Driver's-Ed ten and two. He took a quick glance, again, at the backseat to ensure all there was well. Behind him, tucked to the top of two grocery bags, were two loaves of Seminole bread, a hearty brick of sharp cheese, Dijon mustard, spicy Capicola, a dozen organic eggs, a few token slices of turkey-bacon, and two porterhouse steaks. Lean and thick. The way Jill liked them. A quart of Captain Morgan rum peaked its seductive neck between the pair of loaves, his reward for a safe journey. Farther back in the rear deck was his zero-degree sleeping bag, a can of lantern gas, and an ice auger.

The auger was newly purchased; its spiral fins sharp, the factory-applied red paint, unscratched. At the top, it had knurled arms like the handles of a pogo stick. At the bottom, below the fins, its tip had a tapered steel screw.

The whole device brought an enormous wine opener into Stewart's mind. Giddy, he imagined a proportionate bottle next to it.

The salesman at the sports store told Stewart that it was light enough to carry a distance and it cut a hole quickly. As the young clerk snatched Stewart's card through the credit box, he looked at his customer's plum-colored packaway jacket, the teal Kennebunk shirt under it, and the gold pen in the pocket of it and asked, "You going fishing?" Stewart said no, the auger was simply an experiment, an exploration tool. "A novelty of work," he said as he wrapped his elbow around it and slid it off the counter. On the way out, Stewart felt the teenager's eyes assess his exit, how he swayed out the doors.

As Stewart navigated the road, the auger lay blanketed at the rear of the car. Few vacationers came to the lake in January. The narrow lane to the lakefront cottages was seasonally maintained; and in the summer months, with random patchiness. A pair of tracings marked the dense road pack ahead as if a wide truck, perhaps two snowmobiles, had formed two curvy furrows. Stewart's car wobbled between the slippery tracks, reminding him of being a small boy at the carnival, riding in the jalopy-car, turning the futile steering wheel, the ride not responding, frustrated that a control greater than his choosing was driving.

Waving at his mother as if he was.

Stewart did possess the power of choice, although when presented with it, he often waivered. As he followed the snow-filled channels, he assured himself that his indulgence of a new car with its all-wheel drive, expensive tires, fog-lights, and heated seats was wise. But then a monthly giant payment bullied his dwarf paycheck, adding agony to assuredness.

He was able to make big decisions such as auto purchases, job preferences, apartment choices, and sometimes, partner separations somewhat readily, letting wise impulse override hesitant consideration. But not always declaratively. Simple, trivial choices summoned the greatest anguish. Selecting an entrée, choosing a greeting card, or buying a shirt were decisions that he felt if made with too much thought would turn into a painful disappointment or a misinterpretation.

"Like this shirt," he'd said to Jill three days earlier as he'd picked at the cuffs, strummed the buttons, and thumbed the collar, modeling it for her approval. "Seems like I stood there forever looking at it. It was a good price, but maybe it's not the shirt for now. Or me. It seemed like the right size. But, today it seems too big and I don't like the color. What do you think? Honestly." Stewart counted upon his best friend to do what was expected, to affirm the choice.

Jill surveyed Stewart's new shirt, poured beer from the bottle into her mug, took a cagey swallow, pretended to read the bottle's label, and asked, "What's Richard think?"

"He didn't see it on me. Just in the package. He had to leave this morning before I opened it." Stewart rocked his drink tumbler, feeling as if Jill thought the shirt as less than well chosen. "He said it looked like a summer shirt. Not for January."

Jill deferred to Richard. "He's right. It does look kinda light." Her beer bottle went back to the bar top. "I wouldn't have worn it here." She looked around the bar. "It'll get stunk up with cigarette smoke."

"Seemed like a good choice at the time," Steward said. "But that's the problem." He paused, checked Jill's attention, "Like other things. My decisions. I'm feeling like I've made some bad ones."

"No way. You mean about the car? It's a great car. And a great buy." She made a thumbs-up next to Stewart's drink. Stewart knew that Jill didn't mean the car purchase. "The problem, Stew, is you seem to be making a lot of them lately. And I know you know what I mean."

Stewart leaned back, "Tell me about it." He trundled the highball glass, and then smoothed a condensate bead down the side. "Some've been blunders and some've been good ones."

"No, they haven't," Jill said. Then, a quick correct, "I mean the bad ones. You've made a lot of great decisions. You quit Marcellus-Hale and came to work for Brewster."

"You're the managing editor. You got me the job, fer-chrissake."

"A good move for you. Marcellus was a pit. I rescued you from that pathetic magazine. Pulled you out of that hole just in time." Jill pressed Stewart's arm, her long fingers rolling on it as if a keyboard, "Relax. It's not about me being your friend. You're good at your work."

"Marcellus might disagree. Now."

Jill, into Stewart's ear, "You know their name's got a terrible rap."

"How's that?"

"Marcellus. Get it? The gas shale and stuff."

"Ha! Comparing Marcellus with pits and holes is an easy simile."

"But I like it," Jill winked.

"I don't think too many people will come up with that association," Stewart said.

"Anyway, that place was dragging you down. I couldn't watch you sink. Everything you were doing was turning up cold. I had to get you a hot job. I'm glad you took it."

"Yeah, to fire from ice." He lifted his drink. "How do you know it'll work out? Think I'll regret it?"

"Regret what? Geesh," she cuffed Stewart's shoulder, "it's just a job."

"I don't know. I've had some recent regrets." Swallowing. "About Richard."

"About Richard!"

"Yeah, for one. Some things are like boomerangs," Stewart sketched his tumbler into an arc, "coming back around, you know."

"Aha. Like Richard. You should be glad he did."

"Yeah. He's kind of pushy."

"Ahhh, bullshit, he's great." As a toast, Jill pointed the bottle's mouth at Stewart. "You guys are good together. You're just a wimp."

"Fuck you," he said, then included the gesture.

Jill knocked it away, "Put that thing down." She tipped the bottle, drained it into the mug.

"Richard's waxing commitment."

"Then do so." Eye-to-eye with Stewart, "What're you afraid of?"

"Falling into it." Ice rattled in an empty glass. Stewart looked away; Jill didn't. Stewart came back, "What about my apartment?"

"What about it?" Allowing Stewart to step away from

the conversational edge. "It's cool and it's a great location." Jill nodded toward the back of the bar, "It's close to here."

"It's kind of expensive. My apartment, that is. And I don't know about a two-year lease." Stewart pierced residual cubes with his swizzler. "And at least for now, until Richard starts pitching in." He stopped stabbing. "And if I really want to be with him. And if we...you know, like stay together. And if I get the advance you said. And my taxes get done. And maybe in the spring I'll—" "And, and, and," Jill interrupted. "Jesus, Stew, let it go. Yesterday's gone. Tomorrow isn't here yet." She tapped Stewart's glass with the stone on her ring finger. A bell sound. "Let's have another."

Stewart couldn't let it go. And when he did, it didn't work right. Jill's advice before and after, even without the brief happy hour, always seemed to make sense with or without the aid the tea-brown melt at the bottom of a glass gave. But to let a thing go? To walk away from it? The finality; the absolution. Stewart couldn't accept an end without the possibility of review. To go back and try again. Pull it up and send it in another direction. Like some of the articles he'd edited; there could always be a re-write, revision. A different ending.

Stewart pitched his glass toward Jill, "Okay. You're up. This time it's your nickel."

Jill ordered. The television newscasted monotonously. They watched it blankly for awhile. Halfway through their fresh drinks, their dinner arrived; pulled pork for Stewart and the grilled steak salad for Jill. Rare, blood drops on the endive. Stewart had ordered his simply by opening the plastic menu and offhandedly pointing at the glossy picture, hoping that ordering in so would illustrate to Jill that he was indeed capable of carefree spontaneity. Although, it was a relatively easy selection without the photo, pulled pork was always the Wednesday special.

As they ate, Stewart listened to Jill relate her recent car repair, Laurie's swing shift—and moods—and the reasons the Sabers didn't make it to the playoffs. Stewart was acquainted with Laurie's humors but couldn't recall a recently broken down car or any of the hockey teams that were going to the Stanley's.

"The Maple Leafs, again," Jill answered. Followed by, "How you doing on those pieces I sent? Any rewrites?"

"Yeah, two of them. Well, three actually, including mine. I'm finished with Howard Larson's piece and the one about the Art-Space project is a draft." Stewart leaned on Jill's stool, "Have you looked at mine?"

She elbowed Stewart back to his place, "Yes." She cocked her head, twisted to face him, sucked a pepperoncini off its shoot, pointed the stem at him, "Jesus, Stewart, ice fishing fer-chrissake. Where are you going to go with that?"

Where are you going to go with that? The ice auger came into mind but it wasn't the time to bring it up. "Hey, it's non-fiction. I'm doing the research. I'm thinking of changing the point of view to first-person narrator."

"Point of view? Yours? Hell, you don't know jack-shit about ice fishing. Any kind of fishing, for that matter."

"You want I should go back and edit columnists?"

"No." Jill turned away, "I want you to give me your work." She raked at the salad, weeded out two dainty slices of all-but-raw filet mignon. Stewart watched as they disappeared between her lips.

He worked at his sandwich, tussled with the wet, saucy meat. Someone at the end of the counter called. Bartender-cook Marty walked past. Jill intercepted him, "Marty, you got any desserts left?"

There were. Stewart asked for his regular; a chocolate peanut butter pie—a specialty of Marty's—and a black coffee. Coffee in the evening did not accelerate him; it calmed him. Its dense, consoling aroma gave him a feeling of conclusiveness to the day. Jill had Schnapps on pistachio ice cream. The green aroma, tang of peppermint, and the mellow of vanilla from Jill's bowl made Stewart consider reordering. Jill tapped on her bowl with a spoon, looked at

Stewart, "You can have some of this too." Stewart said that's okay. Jill stirred the ice cream, "It mellows out the meal. Good way to wrap up the day."

Jill came back to Stewart, "So, in the ice fishing story, you say there's this guy in this ice hut talking with the other fishermen. He's telling them about what?"

"Science. Elements changing in state. Water, ice; gas, liquid. Matter in motion; matter in pause." He turned his coffee mug.

"They're going to get all of that out there on the ice?"

"Sure. I think so." Stewart brought the coffee mug to his lips, gazing straight away, Jill saying nothing, just looking at Stewart's coffee sipping, rolling the spoon in her bowl, a tiny dollop to her mouth, studying Stewart's profile. Sensing her stare, Stewart turned to Jill and tried to project a hard line decisively, "I'll show two worlds, the air above, the water below. The ice, a chord between them." He pictured the deep water below, the hard ice that lay on top, the space above inside the fishing hut as if it could be seen as a sectional drawing of a house—the basement, the flooring, the room above. In concept, not yet something to read. He described it some more, without the auger metaphor, but became increasingly aware of Jill sensing vagueness. He switched, "So, boss, what've you been reading?"

Jill brightened, as if she'd been wondering what had

taken him so long to ask. "Something by someone Leslie Stang sent to me. Did you meet Leslie yet?" Stewart shook his head. "Oh, no?" Jill considered a moment. "Anyway, it's about Houdini. Remember the magician?"

Stewart repeated slowly, "Houdini." Jill repeated it too, then offered more details.

"This is fiction?" Stewart asked, still not thinking he'd heard correctly; Jill always working on non-fiction. "The truth," she'd say, emphasizing her coyness on the cliché, "is stranger than fiction."

"No, dear." She smoothed his new shirt, "Well, sorta. He's amazing." Now more animated, she excavated a spoon into a hill of ice cream, "Houdini, not the author." Then set the spoon away. "He could get out of anything. There's this scene where he's dropped into the Hudson River while locked inside a crate. First, they put him in a straightjacket, put him inside the crate, then they wrap it in chains and a crane lifts it above the river." She reached and wiggled Stewart's collar, chuckling, "Like what they should do with your ice fishing fella." Stewart frowned.

Jill went on with the story, diverging from the river escape scene, going on about Houdini's erratic lifestyle, telling about Houdini's previous escapist performances, more about his upbringing, his peculiar brother, and Houdini's nickname, "Harry Handcuff Houdini," Jill said, jauntily.

But Stewart was still back with Houdini in the sealed crate scene. The vision of a box wrapped in chains, the plunge through ice, Houdini's attempted getaway... each played in the back of his mind like the TV on the wall, not fading away. "Did people watch?"

Jill, taken aback, a skeptical posture, uncertain if Stewart had been listening, "Of course, sure they did. That was the trick. To see if he could break out of something they thought he couldn't get out of." Jill overstated it, as if Stewart had missed the obvious. "Of course there was an audience." Jill moved her bowl an inch, continued, "A crane picked up the crate and dropped it into the frozen river. Then he's supposed to come up through a hole in the ice."

"He wasn't in the crate the whole time, right?" Stewart felt as if Jill was leading him, guiding him into some kind of coincidence. For her to tie together the subjects of his new story about a man fishing on top of the ice and Houdini under the ice didn't seem accidental.

"That's the illusion," Jill said, waving her spoon like a wand. "You'll just have to read the script." Two young women came up to the bar, ordered drinks from Marty, and then went for a table. One with spherical facial features and short, curled-in hair. The second, taller than the first, had an angular face, long hair tucked back with barrettes, the way Jill kept hers. Jill paused, watched them order. Stewart noticed Jill follow the taller one's saunter, her pant pocket arches clutching back and forth, tight and empty. Legs like Jill's.

"Anyway," Jill acted as if she wanted to finish the narrative quickly, tapping an empty spoon against the bowl, "the safe plummets to the bottom and it lays there bubbling with Houdini trapped inside." Jill swallowed another spoonful, dug another from the bowl. "Then he swims out."

"Up through the hole? How does the author know this," Stewart asked, wondering that a story with an illusionist character might have an illusionist author.

Jill watched as the two women racked the pool table. Distracted, she tells Stewart, "He explains it later." Jill checked a pool shooter's aim, then turned to Stewart, "He swims away from the safe and tries to get to the top. But when he does, he gets lost and can't find the hole above. But that wasn't part of the trick. He starts frantically clawing at the undersurface, looking for it. All he can see is ice above him."

"Where's the—" A cue ball shattered the rack.

"Just a minute." The spoon clinked into the empty bowl; she faced away from the pool table. "So he finds these small air pockets and can catch quick, water-logged breaths. He's panicking, drowning. Until something weird happens." Jill folded her arms. "Then it gets kind of flakey for a couple of pages. Houdini hears his mother calling him. He's been spending a lot of time trying to get in touch with his dead mother. After she'd died, he got obsessed with the supernatural and met with a lot of spiritualists. But none of them could get his mother to speak to him. Not the way he wanted."

Stewart held his coffee mug out while Marty refilled it. Jill handed Marty her empty bowl. "Then, while he's under water, he heard his mother singing to him; she guided him up toward a different hole and he climbs out of that one. But he's way downstream and the crowd can't see him." Jill looked at Stewart. Stewart was facing Jill, wide-eyed; he blinked. Jill unfolded her arms, "Houdini walks across the ice, bows, and raises his hand like his appearance from another ice hole was part of the show." She reached for a hair barrette, "Do you want to read it or not?"

"Send it over when you're done. I'll read it," Stewart promised. It was a meager pledge and without complete truthfulness or full commitment. "But I'm busy." Nevertheless, the account of a man plunging through ice, lost underneath it, presented a foreboding allure, as if Jill had wandered into his head and come across his confidential plan.

"Let's call it a night," Jill said. She asked Marty for the check. "Work tomorrow, and all that." Marty set the check plainly.

"I got it," and Stewart pinched it off the bar top. Jill allowed. They got their coats and headed toward the door. Stewart told Jill, no he didn't need a ride home, he'd walk, "Remember, I'm close now." Between the coat rack and the front door, Stewart began a secret deliberation. Perhaps this Friday, the day after tomorrow, would be the time to go to the lake for the weekend. He continued contemplating until they walked to the door. They stepped outside. The falling snow, the quiet of the street, the relaxed cocktails, the warm meal cozying in his stomach and the electrifying chill of the night air influenced his decision. Stewart turned to Jill, held her by the coat. "You know what?"

"No. What?"

"I want to go up to the camper this weekend. It's a long weekend. We're off Monday. Martin Luther King Day and all that. Richard said he won't go there in the winter anyway."

"You said he's out of town." Jill curled her coat collar, jangled her car keys, looked up at the snowfall. "This weekend. Now?"

"Yeah. This Friday," Stewart pulled his ski-boggan

over his ears. "We'll take off early and stay until Monday. Ask Laurie, too."

"She's on call." Jill put her hands into her pockets, "I don't think I've got the time to take a full Friday off. I took too much at Christmas." She shook snow, "Besides, I gotta see the pecker-checker Monday."

Stewart didn't ask about Jill's medical appointment. Jill explained, "Not everyone has that holiday, including my doctor." Jill looked toward her car. "So, I'd have to go home Sunday night." She dangled the keys in Stewart's face, "Gotta go. I'll let you know tomorrow. At work. See you then."

"I'll take it as a yes, then."

"A maybe."

Stewart knew that Jill would say yes. That pleased him. He knew that Jill liked the camper. She said she liked its frugal lodging, the nothing-to-do-but-hang ambiance. The notion that they'd all gone in and bought it together. "It's bi-financial," they kidded. Stewart was also pleased that spontaneity was at hand. An unplanned event, planned. A logical impulse. Fortuity. A winter getaway. Two friends, a double-dare.

A double-dare for Stewart; work and research. Challenge and trial. A walk on the ice. Drill a hole with the auger. See the water underneath.

For most of an hour, he'd been the only motorist on the secluded road to Lake Chatumn; unheard of during the summer. He'd passed a car out on the paved, plowed highway but the last car he'd seen was the one parked in front of lonesome Kozy Korner Beer & Video. The store was a marker. It was at that point cell phone coverage ceased. If he needed to make a call while at the camper, it meant driving two miles out to the store.

Radio signals were weak out in the lake country, and if there were a station, it would not be one to which Stewart would listen. He'd forgotten to load music programs into the player in his new car. That gave him nothing to do but mind the road, listen to some reckless country-western music and get to the camper. The interior of his new car had a subdued hush. The engine noiseless. Except for the crackling sound of an imperceptible station, the rock-like grind of tires on ice, and the muted passage of time, he'd driven in pensive silence. His brooding enabled a succession of thoughts to flurry, not unlike the snowing against the windshield, around in his head. He considered that maybe he should've stopped and called Richard at Kozy Korner, but he was probably still in flight. He ought to have called Jill, when he was in cell phone range back then, to check on her progress. Or, maybe he shouldn't have left work so early, being new at the office. And, maybe the power was out for the entire campground, making finding his camper space difficult. Maybe this whole go-to-the-camper-in-January was foolhardy. Maybe the snow wasn't going to stop. Perhaps the ice wouldn't be strong enough?

The car heater blowing made his nose run. He reached for a hankie, blew, and the clearing seemed to purge the wave of unanswerable queries.

The day was hurriedly darkening; the sun was low and faltered between the falling snows. Stewart squirted the last drizzle of washer-fluid over the crystallized windshield creating a translucent, cut-glass mosaic too difficult to see through but stunning enough to enjoy. Shadows washed in behind his headlamp beams. He scraped a porthole through his frosted side window and watched through it, hoping the flat spot on the hill above the camper would soon appear.

As he steered, or piloted, he thought about Jill. Would she find her way along the dark, unmarked road? Usually they rode together, when they'd worked separately. Jill had stayed after Stewart left work. That was fine. It was how Stewart wanted it, some secluded time, unaccompanied for a few hours, a hermit. A solitary winter explorer. At the same time, Stewart looked forward to her arrival later. Her companionship would dispel the loneliness of an entire weekend alone.

In the darkness ahead, the wider space at the edge of the road for camper parking appeared. He pulled in. He checked to see that he was off the road, although he knew it was unlikely another vehicle would pass. The snow tracks behind him were disappearing. Radio static sizzled. He shut the engine off. The headlights' beams remained. They shined bright, aiming level over the embankment and across the shadowed treetops. Two white rails, horizontal and tangible, compelled Stewart to imagine shimming along them, to drop from them through the trees, avoiding the tricky path and a possible dangerous slide into the camper.

The muffler hissed in the packed snow. He enjoyed his new automobile smell, made more robust by heated, circulated air, like fresh clothes from the dryer. When he moved, his parka rustled with static, as if just taken out of that clothes dryer. He was comfy and snug inside the car, up on the road bank, above the cabin, out of the snow, in his insulated coat. The car's rear deck could fold out into a comfortable recliner. The contrast of the restful silence inside his car consoled him against the raucous cackle of last Wednesday's bar night, the fracas of the morning's office work and tension of driving. The late afternoon drive in bad weather exhausted him. For a moment, he considered reclining; he'd have a chat with Captain Morgan and wait for Jill. Perform the experiment in the morning, with Jill. To satisfy her, he'd brought along her Houdini manuscript. He could read it in the car while relaxing. He'd begun reading it, the exposition about the strict rabbi father, Houdini as a nine-year old trapeze artist and the foibles of his disorderly brother. Stewart had thumbed through the upcoming sections looking for the icy Hudson River chapter, but did not find it. He wondered if he had the whole story; Jill may have extracted certain pages. Stewart knew that Jill was aware of the irrational ambition and he felt sure she had used the narrative as a teaser, holding Stewart captive purposefully, but he had intentionally not shown it. It was on the cold, sobering walk home that Stewart worried, fixing the image of breaking through ice against his daring and naïve plan.

The dome light timer clicked and the headlights switched off, dousing all into a black, profound void. The immediate blindness startled Stewart, plunging him again into doubt whether this camping trip—this late, this cold, this time of year—was wise. He looked to see the lake; nothing but chalkboard darkness. All he could see was the lowering clouds and an overturned moon drifting above the callous horizon like a capsized canoe.

Vacillation passed and he stepped out of the car.

When he did, the dome light returned. The reminding ting-ting, ting-ting of the ignition bell, so far out there in the empty woods, chimed an incongruous warning. He plucked the key and tucked it under the seat. The frivolity of hiding the key to the sole car within miles inspired a buoyed whim; he left the doors unlocked and made ready to walk to the camper.

By the time he'd crowded all the groceries into one bag, tucked the brandy near the top for easy access, and arranged his overalls, boots, gloves, socks into his backpack, and arranged the auger—a bulked up trekker with a huge cork screw—the dome light went dark again. He removed a small flashlight from his parka, pointed the dim beam down the embankment, and headed toward the camper. He used the narrow tube of light like a blind man's cane to guide him through the stalking darkness.

Ahead of and below him, perched in a wooded cove neatly surrounded by silhouetted pines, was the camper. It was the lone structure at that end of the lake. The others, further away and around the bend, were settled on flat lawns that stretched to the lake's edge. Other than one boozy New Year's trip a year before, he and Jill had never been to the camper during the winter. Not hard winter. Not by themselves. It had been a temperate, cramped and co-ed weekend then.

Stewart descended the slope in a wide, sidestep progression here in the summer, a path could be followed. He stepped between towering trees, the auger twisting between his arms.

As Stewart passed under them, a sinister presence slipped from behind the trees and followed him. All day the shadowy phantom had remained entombed in the lake's frozen surface, patiently eluding snow clouds and intermittent sunshine, languishing until sundown. When dusk arrived, it escaped from the ice-marbled lake, climbed the cold banks and lurked behind the pines concealing the camper, and awaited Stewart's arrival.

At the bottom of the hill, he kicked through snow until he came to the trailer steps. He set his pack downhill, set the auger against the porch rail, tucked the flashlight between his cheek and shoulders, and fidgeted the frozen lock open. Once inside, he turned the sole light on—a battery lamp. The electricity was out, as expected; power was a summer thing. A light glowed reluctantly out of hibernation, then, warming to company, showed a cheery welcome. He pulled the kerosene heater from under the table, checked its level, and lit it; the tiny, orange-warm companion danced for him.

Stewart, roused by his safe arrival, celebrated the moment and organized the cabin. He'd been looking forward to it since its concept three days ago. The irksome holidays were over. Challenging work was beckoning—hence the office agreement to take time off, now. Richard was in Hong Kong again. His father was well gone to Florida with his new wife. But it wasn't Christmas celebrating, his writing job, Richard's plans, other people, or even insipid decisions from which he escaped.

It was the fear of entrapment. For months, he'd been feeling that the course his life was taking was not the one he'd chartered, that it'd fallen through a hole and was sinking and he, just watching. Unable to rescue it. Winter in the city was desolate. The gym was closed for extensive remodeling. Richard seemed to be career blinded, but wide-eyed with amour. Stewart's new job ensnarled him with strait-jacket assignments, and idiot tasks.

Evasion and avoidance were not among Stewart's qualities, but the notion of anywhere but here prompted him to move. The drive out to the lake made him feel exotic and adventurous. A secreted weekend would be an excellent way to disappear, to break away from workaday familiarity and the routine of relationships. His new car, a new steady boyfriend and a new apartment all helped, but they did not take away his inner ennui.

There was that other thing, too—the lake ice. He wanted to walk far on the frozen lake, to go out at night, alone. It was a private challenge, a mysterious drive that lay hidden on the underbelly of his dull routine. He did not know how to explain it to anyone without it sounding like a dim-witted dare. "It's research," he'd told Jill. "Are you fucking crazy," she'd replied.

His friends talked about being near the edge. For Stewart, the edge was going out on the ice. In his ice-fishing story, he said that if you went out on ice at night, chopped a hole, and set a lantern at the edge, fish would swim to the opening. He imagined sparkling fish floating inside a crystal ball. He'd have to see. That's what he wanted to do: peer over the edge and look into another universe.

But before he did, he'd have to prepare. He uncorked the brandy, set the filets in the sink, checked the propane stove, took blankets out from the cupboard, opened the curtains—to let Jill see the lighted windows and in case it was sunny in the morning—dusted two coffee mugs, tucked the bread into its box, and filled the gas lantern, every once in awhile returning to the kerosene heater for a blast of heat followed by a nip of brandy, like a busy hummingbird.

When the heater warmed the small kitchen to the point where his breath did not cloud, he wrote a note. Jill: There's brandy. Don't let the water freeze. Don't let the heater go out. I'm out on the lake. I'm cool. It's safe. Stewart. He stuck it against the window. He shook his head at the silliness of putting his name at the end of the note. Who else?

He pulled off his parka and stepped into the heavy, oversized canvas coveralls, stiff with newness. The battery clock said 6:20. He lit the gas lantern. He cinched the strings on the coverall hood, stuffed his mittens into the back pockets, and looked out the black window for headlights, wondering if Jill might arrive early, but hoping for her tardiness. Jill would try and talk him out of it. Or worse, chaperone him.

He opened the door and hung the lantern on the railing. He squinted at the opaque thermometer: twenty-two degrees. He was glad it was a still night; a chill wind would drive through the camper walls like needles through thin cloth. He patted his overalls as if checking for leaks. He unhooked the lantern and held it up against the night. The flare shocked the darkness backward, but not far. As he walked, the lantern swayed back and forth, as if it were a scythe slicing the night, making tree shadows dance like drunken demons. Stewart drew in a deep, razor-edged breath. It had been a long car ride. He'd had two coffees on the way and a several generous sips of brandy in the camper. He'd put off the unavoidable as long as possible. He set the lantern behind him, removed his mittens, and peed into the snowy darkness.

Just as he zipped up, he heard the sharp crack of a breaking branch, followed instantly by a hurried, rattling above him. Up by his car. Whatever it was clattered aside the bank, and after still moment, departed silently into the black night, out toward the lake. He stood a moment listening. No sound. He lifted his boot and turned and when he did, he tipped the lantern. The flame extinguished. Overhead, snow clouds were breaking apart, making it seem as if the stars behind them were drifting and all else was motionless.

He started the flame again, brightening it to its fullest. The black obscurity fled. He drew up his mittens. He hoisted the ice auger, tucked the handle under his elbow, affecting a hunter carrying a gunstock, re-adjusted the auger handle again to imagine himself a geographic explorer, not a hunter, a less intimidating posture, and set out for the lake. High up, the moon squinted through shifting clouds. Snow crushed underneath.

He calculated the lake ice to be about three inches thick—how or why, he didn't know, just a guess. He'd watched the weather news on TV. Earlier that evening, as he drove around the northernmost point of the lake, he'd seen fishermen in their plywood icehouses, far away, out on the ice. He watched them shuffle across the big flat ice, back and forth, checking their fishing rigs, like moving punctuation across an otherwise blank page of white paper. If it's safe for those guys, he'd thought, it'll be safe for me. By nightfall, he'd reasoned, it could freeze up to six inches; plenty thick enough to support his body weight and gear. He had an extra pair of wool socks in case his insulated boots leaked. Stewart hiked toward what would be the shore in summertime.

For a second time, the startling clamor, but now as if an armload of firewood was dropped. It had come from a void many yards beyond, then it was gone. After that, an approaching vehicle followed by the sound of galloping— perhaps an animal fleeing? At first, the vehicle sound was muffled by the snow, then a staccato of headlights, then the timbre of ice under tires, steel grinding glass. Perhaps Jill, not seeing the turn-off, missed the cabin? The vehicle passed, then silence. It did not return.

He continued toward the lake. He found a path through the trees, made deep by thawed groundwater run-off, and he walked at its edge, away from the wet center. At the end of the path, he came to the lake ice. It was deserted, no ice fishermen at this end. He tightened his suit zipper, fixed the leather straps under his cap, feeling now like an anxious pilot. The mysterious clatter, the unidentified motorist, the edge of light and shadow, the possibility of the ice, the bulk of the auger, all made his imagination cagey.

He took his first step. Then another. Afterward, wider strides to avoid cracking the ice. A moon-white lake stretched out beyond him. The glass-sharp air pressed into his eyes, forming magnifier tears. The Big Dipper leaned upward, cocked as if ready to catch what Stewart might throw into its scoop. Perseus was a group of tiny perforations in a black-velvet sky. Orion, with his colossal belt and sword, guarding the sky against the attack of star lions. Stewart felt at one with the stars—the ice beneath his feet, a flat of clouds.

Soon, he walked more assuredly but worried he had dressed too warmly. At the gym in shorts and T, he weighed 155 pounds. A lightweight boxer. Out on the ice, in his oversized canvas snowsuit, wool underwear, and flannel shirts, with auger and lantern, he'd become a formidable sumo wrestler. The note he'd left behind on the door began to seem like a last-will-and-testament. He pushed across the ice further, gathering courage. He turned south toward the center. Toward Crest Point.

The ice was covered with a confection of light snow and that somehow eased him, making it seem as if he were out on the solid ground of a parking lot rather than a floating surface. After several yards, he selected a place to stop.

He pushed the snow away with his boot, set the lantern away, placed the auger down next to it, knelt, and brushed open a circular space. Opening a window. It revealed a smoky, mysterious crystal. He knocked at it—the flat sound of a hollow, wooden chest.

The dimming light of his Coleman lantern gave off a soft whisper. He pumped it several times; it brightened. Crouching closer to the ice, he placed the lantern at the opening's border. To see deeper, farther within, he took out his small flashlight, cupped his mittens into binocular shapes around the flashlight lens, and peered into the iced porthole. He saw thousands of tiny bubbles locked inside the ice, a hand-mirror held to the stars above. He waited for fish to appear.

Stewart felt he was looking into the glass globe of a continuing universe; far above—he was sure there might be—a person like him who also peered down at his world through another frozen portal. Perhaps not a person exactly like him, but one who understood his circumstances, his condition. Saw it in the manner he did. Might know future events. The ones he did not.

No fish appeared. Disappointed, he rose. He gathered the auger and lantern. He snugged his mittens, pocketed the flashlight, secured his ear muffs, and continued walking. The crusty snow cover, the brittle ice, the crunch of boot soles, darkened his previously imaginative mood.

When he came close to the round of Crest Point, he stopped and listened to the frozen silence. He stood the auger and rested against it. He surveyed the wide landscape with his flashlight. Last summer, this was the watery place through which ski boats whooshed and sailboats slipped. It was water of inflatable raft and floating tubes.

This was the water from which he and Richard fled as Jill and Laurie ran quickly behind them to catch up. Then, all safe inside the camper, the thunder stormed, the lightning shattered, white caps whipped, the naked wind whistled, and Stewart and Richard watched it, snuggled together in terrycloth covers. This was the same water that when summer ended, it rested beneath autumn's stippled, saffron leaf blanket. Then, winter came, like the one heavy down on Stewart, and all motion ceased, sealing all instance and remembrance, arresting it, freezing those times in a dense capsule. Stewart felt as if he was standing on an opaque slab of time.

He held the auger aside and stood it on its point and it in the light of the lantern, studied the balance of it. He gave it a short spin. Absently, he decided to see if it cut a hole as suggested by the salesperson. He worked the handle clockwise. The screw point twisted into the ice. He turned the handle again. The sharp blade rotated behind it, quickly shaving an icy crumble, just as promised. He turned it again—a drill bit cutting—winding a perfect circle. Then some more. It swirled deeper and with it, bits of rime wound up the spirals. Captivated by its action, Stewart twisted the handles harder. It drove farther into the ice, the blade edges pulling downward, digging a round, shallow hole. The sight of it alarmed him. What if water gushed upward? He reversed the screw and backed it out. The auger took on a suspect appearance with a dubious purpose. It became a clumsy accessory, a daft research tool. Another rash purchase with humiliating remorse. The exaggerated screw blades with their precarious spirals, the sharp edges, the cumbersome handle, its absurd purpose. He threaded it between his arms, embarrassed to be seen with something so terribly insensibly incongruous, as if he'd brought a lawn chair to an art gallery. And the jeopardy of his venture, it now seemed foolish to drill a hole through the same surface that kept him above the water.

The lantern's flaming brightness made the night too edgy. He turned it down. The moon was a backlight. He readjusted the auger. He continued to walk, more shuffle and slide than walking, toward the peninsula of Crest Point.

He was close to that point when he heard a tinkling, a distant patter. He lifted his hood muff and turned an ear toward the sound. It mimicked hysterical laughter. Clearer, without the muffs, it became a slapping and smacking. The wet sound of ice cubes at the bottom of a glass. He quickened his pace and headed for the unseen source. He imagined water splashing. Then, more puzzling, a diving sound. An irrational scene invented in the shadows ahead of him; were fools swimming? The moon slivered above but did not offer clarifying light. He moved nearer and as he approached what he thought was the source he slowed, stepping more cautiously, tiptoeing, as if quick walking would stir more commotion. Another splattering noise, now more of a knocking and sloshing. He thought he heard a crack. The thrill of anxiety rose up through him as if driven from his boots. He became keenly aware of being on a frozen lake.

  Heeding that prudence, he widened his course as he neared the shoreline. He remembered there were small creeks that fed the lake, especially at the areas around Crest Point. He supposed that even on a terribly frozen night, water could be running which might thaw though the ice into dangerous, inky pools. He heeded that speculation and kept a distance away, staying on the open, firmer ice, but his curiosity of the unseen, of that dark shadow, drew him closer

  After much hesitant step and check, Stewart arrived

at Crest Point, where the trees were smaller and the silhouette of the shoreline more visible. He saw an open ring of broken ice the size of a large wading pool, the kind obnoxious children played in while he and Richard lounged at the adult end. The water churned inside, but it was not full of children.

A brown, formless bulk splashed in the center. He quickened toward what he'd imagined was hysterical laughter. Coming yet closer, the sound was not at all comical. It was a convulsed, terrified whine that came from a thing desperately trying to reach for the broken edge. A drowning silhouette of panic. The ungainly figure appeared to be using sticks to pull itself out. It hammered at the icy edges like a manic xylophone player. The horrific scene was punctuated by a tenor shrill, a call of terror.

Assured with adrenaline and blinded from judgment, Stewart hurried to the watery pit. He came up to a few yards of the hole and stopped. The creature made every attempt to grab at the icy perimeter, but the sticks it was using would fall back into the water and the brown form slipped beneath the surface. For a noiseless moment, the water stilled. Then, a showery explosion, a lunging turbulent swirl, and the clawing resumed. When Stewart came within five feet of the water's limit, the creature halted, shaking. The moon's sporadic light gave the quivering water an aluminum glisten.

Guardedly, Stewart walked clockwise around the edge. The thing stalked him. Then alarmed at his nearness, it defensively hooked its sticks onto the jagged ice, innately on guard, prepared to meet its attacker. Rippling water sparkled down its back. Now the form had a head and on its head were amber branches covered with crusted ice. It had eyes. Intimidated, wild ebony eyes. They followed Stewart, watching him from an unfathomable bleak, hollowed out place. From its mouth came rapid gulps. Breaths. Throttling steam from nostrils. It was a deer. A large buck. The sticks, its legs. Spindles wrapped with hair. The brown bulk, a carpet of ragged fur. The amber branches, ten points of boney thorns. The deer jolted.

Stewart leapt backward, nearly slipping on water washed from the hole. He took a step forward, then back because his movements made the drowning deer panic anew, convinced that Stewart was the cause of its suffering. It beat and struck its way a quarter-turn around the hole, stopped and turned to face Stewart.

They paused in a timeless space, both needing to evaluate the menace before them. Stewart came to see a handsome creature that, presumably, had tried to cross the lake when fate seized it.

He saw a velvety face, a stunning rack of antlers. An

elegant, proud animal, before the deceiving water swallowed it. The captured buck returned Stewart's stare with what he perceived as primeval, raven eyes. Then pleading. Then suspicion. Stewart looked down at himself, how he might appear to the deer: he was a lumpy monster, a primordial tormentor, standing unnaturally, towering from above. Stewart felt the auger under his arms, the hanging lantern, the muffs on his ears, his oversized mittens, and saw himself as a glowing cyclops wielding a twisted club. He wanted to apologize, to make clear that he was simply a human man.

They watched each other in a time without measurement, but in those mysterious moments, a reckonable awareness overcame Stewart—to perform a rescue attempt. But how? The buck seemed to detect Stewart's contemplation, as if waiting for death, or to be saved by a mistake.

While staring at that midnight water with the deer clinging to the ice, Stewart felt himself drowning, drowning in helpless passions. He suffered the buck's desolation, feeling just as trapped and incompetent. He was caught between an act to help or to stand back and allow nature to take its course. Then there was the matter of his safety. The outcome of attempting to pull a wildly panicked deer from freezing water had no certain ending.

Free will, fate, tragedy, and transformation...did they

have any logical sequence? Or were they a succession of chaos? Could he change the course of this event? Until Stewart had come upon the deer, he'd found the courage to make all of the decisions in his life, with mild reluctance. Some of them he had pondered slowly, with deliberation. Others he had made too quickly and flustered, as if he were a frightened passenger on a sinking ship, clambering for the last lifeboat. If he had made a decision at all. Idiot problems ensnared him with their superficial options, which he enabled further, by ambivalence. All trivial, compared to the dying creature. How many times had he heard Richard say, You *know, Stewart, it's not a matter of life or death.*

When Stewart attempted a particular outcome, the situation often found a conclusion of its own. One where the ending differed substantially from how he'd planned. Now, as he stood at the ice's edge, contemplating the opportunity to which he felt compelled to respond, or not to respond, he wished he had Houdini's power to carry it out, that whatever he was going to do would magically produce the desired result, an illusionary trick.

The deer supported itself with both front legs on the ice. The clouds parted, allowing the radiant moon to reveal a transformed scene. Stewart knew then, without question and with absence of reason, he had to save the pitiful creature.

He hurried toward the shore, acting on impulse rather than plan, absentmindedly still clutching the auger. Using the lantern as a headlight, he scanned his path. He did not know there was a narrow band of thinner ice between him and the land until he came upon the black-puddled shadow of it. It could be dangerous... how deep was the water? He went to its edge and pushed hard to jump across the gap, but he missed and crashed into cold, calf-deep water. Stewart thanked the miraculous reason why the lantern did not submerge and remained shining. He stepped out of the water back onto the ice, but another chunk broke away like rotted flooring. Both boots now full of water, he used the auger as a staff, pushed up, grabbed a frosted bush, pulled out, and stood on the shore frenzied with panic. He spotted a fallen tree whose branches resembled a hayfork. He turned the lantern brighter, set it down, and using the auger now as an axe, began chopping at a tree limb. Fiercely, he hacked at it, whacking away skinny branches and shortening thicker ones. Each ring of the metal auger blade synchronized with his frantic, thumping heart until he'd cut a long, curved, ladder-like shape from the tree.

Avoiding where he had fallen moments ago, he dragged the limb around it and onto the ice. The water in his boots was Novocain. He considered the spare wool socks, warm and thick and dry, but there was no time for that now.

The deer had stopped thrashing and seemed to be waiting, as if it recognized its rescue was underway. Stewart pushed the makeshift ladder toward the deer, rolled it, then pushed it closer and closer. The buck snorted and moved away, threatened. Stewart shoved the limb again, beyond the edge, into the water. He sat, put his foot against it, and gave a strong heave, envisioning the ladder reaching the deer, where it could climb the rungs and leap to safety. Stewart saw confusion in the wild, dark eyes. Looking deeper, he saw fatal acceptance.

He ignored that and cried, "Take the ladder!" The deer remained motionless, staring at Stewart. Now Stewart shouted, "Damn it! I'm going to save you, if you let me!" With both legs, he kicked the branch firmly. It slipped just a few feet forward and hung limply over the edge, like a lifeless hand. Stewart's kicking made the buck clamor away. Stewart moved closer to the hole; he could touch the water. Disregarding his fear of being so dangerously near to the fractured edge, he crouched and grabbed the stock of the limbs. By hand, by hope, and by new strength, he turned the whole branch toward the deer and over the edge, into the water.

It rolled, turned to a different angle, floated, and stopped unhelpfully, not reaching the deer. "Damn it," Stewart yelled, frustrated that his efforts were falling short. Finally, oblivious of his own peril, he stood and went to cracked edge of the ice, sat at the rim, and gave the limb one last Herculean shove. It swished forward, and with what seemed like imminent success stopped next to the buck, nearly leaning on it, the thickest part of the limb resting safely and securely on the ice's edge. Shaken, shivering, Stewart watched and waited.

Like a desire he'd never experienced, he wanted to see the buck rise from the water, climb safely up the limbs, stand up stately, shake away the clinging ice, bow his antlers gratefully, and gallop, unharmed into the woods. Just as Houdini had. The wand waved, the magic performed, the stunt completed successfully.

Instead, inexplicably, the limb slowly rolled backward, counter to the direction intended. As it turned, it caught the buck's antlers. The deer misunderstood the ladder rescue for an enemy's attack and burst in the opposite direction, away from the frightening branches, its eyes wide with terror. "No!" Stewart shouted. The deer splashed to the other side, trying to flee the rolling branches lashed to its head, and when it came to the opposite edge, it made an astonishing change in motion. Shocked and frightened, it lunged direly into the middle of the water where the thickest limbs were girdled closest to the center of the trunk. There was an eruption of water, a brawl of legs, an arching of back, and a blur of antlers as it attempted to battle the wooden forks. They rotated faster, and like a hamster in a wheel, the deer scuffled inside it.

Stewart leapt at the water and tried to stop the rolling spoke by grabbing at the trunk. As he leaned, his hand broke off a piece from the iced edge and his arm plunged beneath the water. Disregarding the frigid wetness, he attempted to stop the limb from turning, but the long, thick branches spun like threshing forks. The branches entwined between the deer's forelegs and spinning faster, strangled around the buck's head. They curved around its antlers, enveloping the creature in a choke of writhing twigs with the terror of two clutched drowning victims.

"My God," Stewart moaned, visions of a chained Houdini wrestling in his mind, "I've thrown it a straightjacket!" The deer struggled uselessly. Stewart, aghast that he had been transformed from hero to torturer, felt he'd caused the deer's drowning. He flopped belly flat, spread outward across the ice like in the pictures he remembered from Boy Scouts, crawled with hazard to the edge. In this final, desperate attempt to stop the churning tangle, his legs kicked over the lantern. It skidded, made an instant bright flash, and then extinguished.

The deer, convinced that Stewart was indeed his ghostly tormentor, tried to escape the death wheel by climbing through its brush trap and out the other side. It kicked some branches away, but another cluster of quick, heavier limbs rolled again like many handles, pushing the deer beneath the water. The large center branch became a gear spoke, grinding into the water like a paddle wheel. The splashing water churned into an icy froth as the deer arched upside out, gasping in a wet, hollow noise.

Stewart reached behind him for the auger, pulled it to him, stabbed it between the turning limb stock and the rim of the ice hoping to use it as a wheel chock, but the momentum was too much. The blades sliced into the branch and pulled out of his hand; the handles broke away an edge of ice and revolved with the tree limb, the auger rotating with the churn of the branches.

Tangled and panicked, with nowhere to go but upward into the hands of its demonic savior, the buck dove underwater, beneath the ice shelf, as if it had seen a deep escape hole and swam toward it.

Without the deer kicking inside it, the tree limb ceased rolling, rocked backward and forward a few times, and slowed to a stop. The churning water quieted. Stewart lay motionless in a numb trance. Time ceased, space collapsed. Silence. The moon, now opaque, migrating between the clouds, its reflection dappled on the threatening water. Icy water droplets from the twigs plunked into the surface.

And then, like the startled lurch made by a horror movie, an inverted deer corpse abruptly appeared beneath the translucent ice. Its antlered head bobbed atop a lifeless buoyant silhouette like a shadow packed of bones. A faint hoof clicking, the ominous thump of body, the knock of skull bumped at the underside of ice, to hear the grave thud of a burdened soul trudging down a wooden stairway was the sound. Stewart recoiled, just as the horror film viewer had. The dusky shadow beneath the translucent ice grew larger. Flat bubbles slithered like silvery leeches, then slowed, then stopped all together; an ill-omened simile.

Stewart crawled dangerously too near to the edge and peered over it. The water stilled. Again, like those in the hole he'd cut earlier on the other side of Crest Point, he saw many tiny bubbles locked inside the ice. He begged that they would somehow bring it, float it to reappear, but they did not oblige. They seethed, then closed.

Steward bawled; the cry of a human siren. But no rescue arrived to the alarm. "Oh, no! No! What have I done?" Aloud. Desperately, numbly. He knelt at a place where the black water and the crusted brink threatened. He reached out unbalanced, rearranging the tangled branches in a feverish quest like a lost man in thick brambles searching for an opening, positioning the thickets thinking that to do so would give the deer another chance to recover. But the searcher could not see its missing among it.

As if in a torturing encore, the shadow from beneath appeared once more, indistinctly, adrift distantly as if a darkened suggestion of something indistinct floating away on an ocean waves.

It faded. It dropped from view with renounced conclusiveness, disappearing as ominously as it had appeared, floating downward, vanishing quietly like the subtle closing mute of theater lights.

Stewart stepped away from the fatal hole, swayed dizzily, and took hold of his lantern—the wick was broken lightless, a thing with an extinguished soul. Using his cold hands, the same as those of a grave digger he grieved, he scooped the little flashlight out of his pocket. Now he flashed the dimming light among the sinking branches, thinking reappearance. All that showed was the outline of branches and the water from them dripping rings on the blackish surface.

In the faint he looked for his auger. It hung out-of-the-way, gouged uselessly into an unreachable far place on a limb. He staggered off the ice, around the gap that had tried to drench him, up the bank that had tried to collapse. Stiff, wet, and with a worthless lantern, but the only thing he was left with, he made his way to Crest Point Hill. He followed a dark path that the weak flashlight beam lead, groping his way by the light of a fickle moon, a dying battery light, and an invisible calling which finally led him without explanation back to the camper.

Jill was not there. Her absence gave the camper a deserted, sunken chill. He checked his cell phone. Its bitter plastic, absent reception bars, blank screen felt as if holding cold granite. He twisted the kerosene heater knob hoping it would bring forth a promising glow, but it did not. It radiated brightly for a brief time, but soon gave off a lonesome heat. He poured cider halfway into a mug, filled the other half with rum. He put on dry socks, but his feet refused to thaw. He thought about driving to that distant store, but drained of all energy, he slumped into bed.

It was midnight until he could pull a warming blanket over his head. Bitter silhouetted deer images haunted; the gray clouds that weighed above, the water that had concealed all pressed heavily against his eyes. At last, he closed them.

He knew he had tried; tried in all that he knowingly could have. He would tell them that he had; them—Richard, Jill. Indeed, he'd made it out onto the ice.

With mercy, sleep came to him as a comforting assuage, convincing him that the drowned deer had nothing to do with his shortcomings, the obvious metaphor too disturbing to acknowledge; even write about. But it was a remorseful solace. The lantern brightened, faded alternately, dimmed, and when Stewart was asleep, the last flame died.

During sleep, a bitter wind carried about, pacing through the woods, it tried to stalk under the door, changed its attempt, then opted to spend the remainder of the frigid night lingering outside, rustling amidst the thickets, scratching at the camper walls like a restless prowler.

When the night peaked with barrenness, the same sinister air that had floated out from the woody shadows when Steward first came to the camper, again crept onto the lake, and becoming a phantom mason, mortared the watery grave solid, sealing it as it was before the deer plunged. The twisted branches, the frozen limbs, thrust upward, fixed like calloused hands, hands that clutched Stewart's auger aloft as if a victory and the auger a spiral trophy.

Sky Diving

Surrendering, Russell advanced mutely toward what looked like what was supposed to be his chair, a terrible chair under a sanitized table inside a windowless office during the Happy Hour-less afternoon. He stared at the wall where the hands on a cheaply replicated choo-choo train clock faltered, the minute hand dangling wearily at 6. Thirty minutes to wrap it up. The hour hand pointed down to the right, as if sighting for him his chair. A tweed upholstered thing, the limp lumbar pad gesturing don't lean against me.

Molly came in, took a chair that seemed to have familiarly about it. It wheeled without effort to the table and she sat into it easily. "Hello, Russell," arms x-shaped on the table, an authentic smile for him, "how did that project finally end?"

"It ended." But far in advance of that end, and not too soon before the divorce dust was about to make its final settlement, Russell was certain—and he was becoming even more certain about it while brooding about that chair over there in the corner of the magistrate's office—that ultimately, most definitely, Yes, sir!—that after all was said and done, there'd be more done than said.

Now seated, "There's always the closeout." Not leaning into the lumbar, "Nothing's over until it hits the ground." While putting his hands out on the table he leaned against the sagging lumbar, trying body language that said he was ready to sign those multiple copies—yeah, those legal-sized papers stacked pompously at the center of the table—apathetically.

Molly did not decode the sign, or didn't need to. From a legal-sized folder she produced her paperwork, pointed them at those on the table, "They are yours."

He reached them over. What was it with attorneys and their legal-sized paperwork? Why can't the son-a-bitches just use regular sized paper? The kind that fits on a letter-sized page; that fits into a right-width folder; that fits into a length-right copier? That fits into a shredder.

A door opened and Molly's attorney came in pushing a well-steered chair. Clearly, his. He glanced at the choo-choo clock. "Okay." He sat, elbows on wide armrests.

Now Russell was diagonal from Molly. He couldn't deny that she looked cheerful, not at all flippant as he'd forecasted beforehand. If compelled, he'd have to confess that her bright short-sleeved blouse, the spruce afternoon-off slacks, the simple barrette clipped askew, willed a pleasant reminiscence.

The attorney palmed the back of Molly's chair. "How are you Ms. Molly?" A warming inflection.

Ms. Molly. Indeed. Molly, the plaintiff. Plaintiff: as written confidently above the VS. on the paperwork under his elbows. The soon to become ex-wife. And, if Russell had surmised the coyly encrypted phone messages that preceded this afternoon's meeting with full correctness, was soon to become Mrs. Margaret Hangstrom—no longer Mrs. Margaret Seastrum; as in Mr. & Mrs. Russell Seastrum. Because her soon-to-be-former and her expected-to-be newer surnames rhymed ironically, Molly's attorney referred to her as Ms. Molly, pronouncing it with such portentous diction that it seemed he did it too officiously, as if a butler. The intonation coming clearer to Russell that Molly's attorney-butler wanted to avoid an erroneous slur-mix of the surnames which might inadvertently reveal his dual representation: divorce/counselor-marriage/officiate.

The attorney shook Russell's hand, then sat at ease into his chair, seated diagonally across the table. Yes, diagonally: Russell at the V-point too focally.

The door opened again. Russell's lawyer, Larry (Larry fer-Christsake. What kind of lawyer goes by fuckin' Larry?) came in and gave the X-shaped pattern equilibrium: lawyer-defendant-lawyer-plaintiff. Larry squeaked his assigned chair closer to Russell, and while he swiveled it into position, stood there too long. Russell leaned obliquely, peering around Larry as if this reluctantly selected teammate-attorney was a late arriving spectator who, as he took his seat on the bleacher, was blocking a good view of the game. The attorney sat. Russell reclined back into the chair feeling that no matter what happened during the game he was going to either miss seeing the hits or fail to spot whether balls fell foul or fair.

Molly's attorney (who, as he distributed all the paperwork, began then to appear more umpire than butler) sat conclusively at the top of the X while he methodically passed pens, files, and papers around the table. During the proceedings, Larry spooled his copies into a tapered roll, which looked too much like a baseball bat for Russell's like. He didn't know where all the baseball analogies were coming from; he's indifferent to the sport.

Nevertheless, the game went on. Russell's last chance was a fly ball that sailed readily into Molly's field. Her attorney caught it, threw it back unhurried, and then everything was over. The adjudicator's tag-teaming finished, the courteous bickering said, the formalities done. With their pens put to rest, the manila folders filled, the chairs pushed back, their shirt cuffs tugged politely, Russell watched his tangible dreams vanish from the desk, brushed away like discarded program rosters swept up by insensitive stadium custodians.

As they did, Molly's butler/lawyer attempted jauntiness, quipping sprightly, "Just like splitting peas in a pod." It came across stiffly. Russell tried a smile but it was unconvincing. Again, trying to express merriness, Molly's butler/lawyer clacked the elastic strap that bound the finished paperwork together with a taut snap, "That's a wrap."

Then at last, the last done was said and Russell hoisted himself out of the detainee's seat he'd occupied for the past eternal hour, during which he'd stared contemptuously at the stupid choo-choo train where the minute hand had suspended tired at 6, and when it finally began to pull itself up and out of the deep vale that had it mired there exhausted, the start was like a slow tram ride up a steep mountain. Unmercifully, the sluggish minute hand made its tired climb, passing over the rounded humps of the 8 as if a pair of high bluffs, and arrived straight up at the 12 and rested there, tired.

12 was the pre-arranged adjournment time, whether resolution was achieved or not. Top of the hour," Molly's butler-attorney chirped. A coo-coo came to mind.

So, decisively, it was now time to leave. As he rose, Russell gave one last odious glance at that interminable chair with its stupor-inducing upholstery and the inebriat-

ed plastic wheels that rolled conversely each time he'd tried to slide forward to sign yet other pages—legal sized, goddamnit—and leaning forward in that woozy chair had made the pen they handed him fall clumsily as if he'd been trying to balance a pole-vaulter's lance between his fingers, which, when it fell,
everyone watched tumble gracelessly off Molly's corner of the desk so that her butler-lawyer had to sidecrawl his own creaking chair to the table's edge, inelegantly bend for it, and pick the naughty pen off the floor, which when after he'd handed it back to Russell snorted like an umpire who had to return a wildly slung bat to its slippery palmed batter.

As Russell made his retiring send-off to the hostage chair, he feigned a humble nod. When he was fully stood, he faced the lawyers which included his own yellowpages-selected Larry-Lawyer. Larry had advertised his profession with Free Service. In the book the italics were in bold, but later, as Larry-Lawyer confessed, it'd been a typo for Fee Service. Russell bowed to Molly, turned sideways, then bid the whole gang farewell. Left the room.

While exiting, a warm and snuggly and mood-raising feeling overcame him. A confirming smile widened that, indeed, very much indeed, there'd been more done than said. But, there was more. And he was happy about it—

smug with content really—that he was thoroughly satisfied that he had actually gotten all and everything he really, really simply wanted: to smoke in bed.

Two longs days, two-hundred too stretched miles, two robust bourbon-brimmed tumblers later, he relaxed. Contented. He rested on the bed of his ascetic apartment, under
the covers, legs bent, head on three firm pillows, comforter pulled to his chest, an ashtray—a cup saucer—propped tippy on a cocked knee, cigarette smoke drifting purposeless.

Indeed, indeed, it was all insensibly enjoyable. Yeah, yeah, he'd had two—well, one more, three—bourbon highballs and a hefty bottle of beer before and after dinner and he held his cigarette maybe too lax between his fingers, and his eyelids were sleepily ajar, but he was defiantly content. At last, the said was done.

He smirked at his perilous activity, imagining tomorrow's headline: "Man's Body Found in House Fire." His hurriedly gathered second-hand furniture would be sifted from the smoldering rubble like found melted things in the coals of a morning-after campfire. His brittle body, too charred for actual identification except for the circumstantial apartment occupancy and license plate tracing, would be found tucked still cozy under stiff-blackened comforters, the tell-tale cigarette pack inexplicably intact in his palm, lighter in the other, as if ready to light up. The reporter's quote from the fire investigator saying that the inspection found, "smoking in bed" the cause of the blaze.

He continued to smoke. His non-filtered cigarette. "100 % Natural Tobacco" it stated as obliquely as the italics on the pack said. His validation to smoke filter-less cigarettes was that he was inhaling something less lethal than those other compound-chemical filter cigarettes, packed with formaldehyde flame retardants, cadmium, butane— arsenic? he wasn't sure—and whatever else was stuffed into the fiberglass end of the cigarette those other smokers breathed. The natural tobacco rolled into his paper tube was grown, harvested, and untreated (at least that's what was implied by Natural.) by Seneca Indians. His rationale for smoking straight tobacco was that it sanctioned him for a special, healthier demise.

Besides, he didn't feel the need to pay attention to that ostrich-necked plastic vase outside his office door where those disreputable filter smokers congregated; puffing with a furious rage while rain and snow tried to extinguish their pleasure. He just walked on by, flicking his non-filtered one into the building entrance pachysandra, haughtily. Confident, from his perspective, that it would burn out quickly, environmentally considerate, without the evidentiary mark a thoughtlessly discarded fiberglass filter would leave as it smoldered conspicuously there on the mulch. Any adverb would do, as long as he didn't have to stub his smoke into the soot-stained hole at the top of the wobbly urn.

There was a small lamp over his bed, a low light in a metal cone clamped askew to the headboard. It shined sideways on his face, screening a shadowy profile against the wall. The light was enough to keep him faintly alert in the event the cigarette fell between the quilting. Through the window at the foot of the bed he could see that nighttime had grown less optimistic. Beyond the glass it was dark; a grey chalkboard night. Inside the neighbor's windows a yellowy dimness glowed behind gauze curtains. He had not yet met the neighbors. He wondered if there might be some blithe youthful woman who might stand behind the curtains, presenting a willowy silhouette: arched breasts, rounded curves, broad hips swaying with the same movement as the languorous smoke drifting from his ashtray.

Of course—no action. He took another arrogant drag. Last cigarette. Then crushed it. He picked the saucer off his knee, set it on the blanket. He thought about getting a bedside table. Sometime. He stared at the ceiling, looked at the book splayed out on the floor. The chipper first-person narrator and the too-much-fun characters were not synchronized with his present sardonic mood. Read it later. He turned off the light.

Abruptly, turned it back on. Where's that brochure? The one he'd read three times after his first two pre-meal bourbons. That third one later, without ice, colluded with the first. Three fingers worth. His amber reading glasses. At first he did not actually read it, he just gazed hazily at the glossy photographs. He was especially baffled at the picture of the young, gleeful couple—probably on a honeymoon fer-Christ's sake—plunging hilariously like stringless puppets, rubber faces flapping at one-hundred sixty miles an hour toward the tiny farm squares thousands of feet below them. Then, after several gulps, he was encouraged by the oblivious frivolity of it all. Skydiving. Now that could be something that might be fun. The sudden risky whim revitalized him like one of his cigarettes. He thought he might just smoke another one, spiteful, in the bed. But boozy sleep was mounting, ensuring with greater probability tomorrow's headline.

He had to pee. Russell pulled the bedsheets to one side and stared at the rumpled creases blankly as if there was some abstraction between them he was supposed notice but didn't see. Not recognizing it put him into a mood that he couldn't identify immediately, leaving him vacant,

Sky Diving

gazing at the sheets absently, making him feel as if he were seated in a waiting room, opening the magazines with no intention to read them, fanning through the pages in case there was. From the folds on the sheets incongruous associations about Molly emerged: how she tucked bedsheets, doubling a hospital fold as if origami; the way she'd recycle magazines, piling them neatly face-up, chronologically, even though they were going to be hauled off by insensitive truck drivers anyway; her unhurried teabag dipping. Caught off-guard by why those memories happened, Russell had a hasty impulse to reach forward and yank the bedsheets back. But he didn't. He allowed the memory to linger, savoring it as if he'd found a long-lost trivial memento in his jacket pocket that represented something wistful.

He did not let the emotive moment set too long. Instead, he pushed up off the bed. But while rising he discovered that the frivolous reminiscence about Molly had unbalanced him and he wobbled on his elbows. Or maybe it was the bourbon? He tugged the sheets, the saucer-ashtray spilled. The gray smudge reminding him of his present state: wife-less. And, without a wife to protest smeared cigarette ashes.

That notion fancied him and he smoothed the ashy smear into the sheet. He made a promise that neither melancholy, nor aggrieved, nor would celebratory marital memories encumber his new-found bachelorhood fun. The ash blemish grew sootier. A lot of fun that'll be washing that out. He wrinkled the top sheet over it.

Yeah, fun. He considered the idea of fun; like it was the stuff seen leafing between his fingers while flipping the magazine pages in that waiting room. Advertized fun, like something one went out and bought some of. Get some on the way home.

The wife: "Hey, honey, can ya stop an' get some fun?"

The husband: "Wadda ya need, sweetheart?"

The wife: "How'a bout a couple-a-pounds worth?"

Shit. He sat fully up out of bed. He looked around the empty room.

Why did fun have to be the Madison Avenue kind of fun, planned and packaged? It seemed like people needed to be told what excitement was by those people who had loud, incandescent teeth; the ones brimming from billboards. He recalled the Jamaican Me Crazy Festival of a couple of weeks ago held downtown, the streets closed off with traffic pylons disguised as rum bottles. Russell walked among it. What use does a white bread-and-mashed potato kind of town have for rum and reggae? He'd drunk some of the rum, joined the event, see if he could find any fun, but it didn't work for him—the rum that is.

Sky Diving

Recently, fun had been like being a blindfolded hostage in the back of a truck. Flexible handcuffs for his comfort. Flexible? Is that what Molly had said back there at the surrender? "Flexible conditions to be determined" by the statutes of court. The spoils of war divided inequitably by that silver-suited generic attorney in that squeaky chair. Sheesh. Right. That was a lot of fucking fun.

Where'd those cigarettes go? Over there on the dresser. He changed his mind, again. Maybe, indeed, he should indeed lay off the smokes.

Somehow Molly's presence hadn't left the room. Her countless admonishments during the remaining days tingled annoyingly, "Harold doesn't smoke."

Harold, huh? Thoughts of her not so recent, lately euphemistic, companion-escort flushed him spiritedly. "Huck", as Russell condescendingly refers to Harold. Tactically. Never to anyone near Huck. Just the boys down at Snuggies. The one's who were buying.

Several months before Divorce Day, Harold personally delivered several potted trees to Russell's house—Molly's landscape plan. He'd brought them in his own car. (A sorry jellybean-shaped thing the same sweetly pastel color as one of them is how Russell recalls it these days.) Russell signed for the plants. Molly bustled them out to the patio. Harold helped her carry the plants around back, careful not to soil his white overalls. Then settling on the plant's arrangement jointly, they shared a Pepsi. Russell kept to his gin and tonic. Molly accompanied Harold out to his car, a momentary chat, an appreciative hug, and then he drove away. A few weeks later he returned with potting soil. Harold had affixed one of Molly's sisterhoodly political stickers to his rear bumper. Seeing it, Russell's first thought was: what's a feed store fellow doing with a perkily pink tie-ribbon-for-something-or-other sticker his goddamn bumper? The full representation of its meaning not dawning on him until much later. Even if he'd let the thought inhabit much space when he'd first seen it, he didn't think he needed to suppose much more about Harold. He was simply Handy Harold, an amusing tag that Molly would have even accepted; a playful nickname for a family friend. In those days, Russell's view on Harold was calmly uncaring, as if Harold was a kite loosed from a broken string—a wafting prospect.

Huck, a nickname deigned for his bucolic personality—his fuddy manner. Harold works at Brindle's Feed N' Nursery. Sells fertilizer, plant seeds, dog food. Manager. Russell's fixed image of Huck is him in a T-shirt; one with no pockets. Russell's never been inside the store, but he has seen Harold in his pressed shirt, "Harold Hangstrom: Manager" pinned rightly over the left pocket. But these days, in Russell's image, Huck sports a pocket-less T-shirt.

Sky Diving

At a time, now gratefully past, Russell and Huck were agreeable acquaintances. Harold persuaded Russell to become a volunteer fireman. Rooky Russell, briefly. He went on two mid-day fires, performed traffic waving. Fire Chief Harold didn't direct traffic. He was certified: state honors; a couple medals. At the firehall Harold played a miserly poker game, sliding his quarter into the ante was as if pushing a manhole cover across the table. Drank Black Velvet with ginger ale. Lots of ice. Never drunk.

Harold and Molly had a relationship, too. Not with liquor or poker, but at church—vestry members. Russell knew the outside of the church, but had no clue about what went on inside. Harold's wife had died a year ago—or, as Russell cogitated on his way out of the magistrate's office that day, maybe two? Thought it was some kind of blood disease; her white cells thinning too weak, or the red one's too strong. It wasn't long after the funeral when Molly began to escort the widower-Harold into bachelorhood with sibling-like deliberation—a resilient sister with her ductile brother. In spite that the appropriate mourning period had not yet elapsed, Harold became a frequent dinner quest. All of that was okay with Russell. Harold had been peripheral ahead of his wife's death, coming for bar-b-que, leaving his wife for her evening rest. One day they drove to Breezewood together and went on the rides. Harold liked the roller-coaster, something astonishing to Russell as he sat on the park bench next to Harold's wife, she blanketed warmly even on that summer day, while Molly screamed with Harold at the loop.

Those were the days when things occurred around Russell in an indiscriminate fashion, evolving inexplicably: unexpected Fiesta-Ware arrived, the happy-green, jolly-red and sunlit-yellow china appearing vibrantly as if a mysterious rainbow; the bag of volleyballs tightly netted in the back of Molly's car; landscape plants multiplied like mushrooms around the deck. The household bills were paid with ambiguity—but, content that they were, he left the envelops uninspected. When he and Molly vacationed, she just handed him his seat ticket. All he cared was that the airplane's beverage cart made frequent stops to it. Huck, too, probably evolved gradually.

Russell scuffed the bedroom floor expecting slippers. No slippers. More absent things from the past.

Yet Huck evolved inexplicably. Russell smirked about the evolution, thought of it unkindly, picturing Huck like a lungfish, slithering onto the beach newly evolved.

Slipper-less, Russell admitted—accepted?—that Harold's appearance likely was substantial, and had occurred well prior to the day Molly had said it was time to move out. Russell, not her. Who knows, Harold could've been standing out there behind the garage, waiting, not smoking cigarettes all these past months. Huck was probably inconspicuously obvious when Molly's sister, Maureen, showed up as a temporary house companion. Allegedly, a mortgage helper. Russell figured Huck was there to help unload Maureen's van. Handy Harold probably got excited carrying Maureen's clothes rack: the silky Japanese housecoats, the skimpy chemises, the strapless sarongs. Probably looked in the dresser drawers. Tie-dyed panties. Thongs. Probably got himself a hard and hefty Johnson. Probably thought he was making a mistake sniffing around Molly. Maureen, a better piece.

She was. Russell liked it when Maureen visited. He liked it that she didn't care, nor knew how to, fold a hospital corner. Russell stood. He jerked the covers against the wall, hiding the soot stain. He scratched at his boxers, turned the lamp to point downward, less brightly, less interrogation-like.

Something about how the lamp light had shined outward got him recalling a time, a dense car ride not too long ago. The lamp light; those headlights at night.

He was driving back from Molly's obligatory Memorial Day office picnic. Actually, he wasn't driving at all. He was a passenger. The always half-empty cocktail glass he'd carried around all afternoon drew suspicions from Molly and at the party's end she insisted he be a passenger. He plunked into the seat, well loosened, next to her. After some front seat meeting-like agenda, listening to her take attendance of conspicuously absent office workers, and that the registrations for the upcoming fundraiser were delinquent, and that the tax assessment appeals on the house were underway and that..."Dammit, Russell, the basement door still gets stuck even if you slam it hard,"...she told Russell she was seeing someone. In a flat, even tone. Seeing someone. Explaining it obscurely, using euphemisms. Russell heard her words, but they didn't make any sense, as if nonchalantly she was telling him how space aliens had come down and washed all the house windows and then sang Christmas carols and then when they were finished, were supposed to go around back and tell Russell that his wife was seeing someone.

What?

Seeing someone? She didn't give out a name. He didn't ask. He couldn't figure out how to make the question come out without sounding stuperous.

Days afterward, how many he couldn't remember, but he had himself a great big chuckle. Then, a great bigger chuckle when Molly revealed it was Harold. Ahhh...Huck! An explanatory moment flashed. Much like as in a murder mystery when the novelist reminds the reader of all the hinted details that hadn't been paid attention to previously in the story. Ah ha! So that's why they left the large suitcase at the waterfront dock, or, why the baseball bat took too long to be identified.

Molly with another man? Was it adultery? No, adultery is for Victorian novels, not mysteries. What about sex? With Huck? The thoughts rattled around in Russell's head like the last hard to get coins from a piggy bank; hard to shake out. Usually, then in time, rarely, did it occur to think of Molly in any sort of sexual way. Sure, she was attractive, might have even fit into her sister's things. In a way she'd come to into some kind of genderless nature, almost willfully. There were times when he'd pondered her sensuality, although resentfully. As he did at the clothing optional beach while looking at her all wrapped-up in a canvas-like single piece swimsuit while other sunbathers languished nude, or in threadlike thongs, or if not naked, en suite with transparent, anatomy-gripping fabrics.

Recalling that beach scene inclined Russell to look once more out the window, at the one across. The curtains remained lightly shaded, but no company. The wishfully silhouetted neighbor must have gone to sleep with the lights on.

He remembered why he'd gotten out of bed. He walked across the room. He peed. Then he remembered the brochure out there in the kitchen.

Molly and Hunk, huh?

Now in the kitchen. He wondered how they did it; how did they plan it? They must have thought about it before doing it, before going all the way. Did they just stand there at the door, together, terrified at the last panicky moment, stopped with uncertainty? Were they unsure of the wisdom of such a thing, not knowing if it was something they really should do?

Or did the affable skydiving instructor just push them out of the plane into the whooshing air? That's how Russell would not want it to happen. Shoved out like when Teddy Wasmund pushed him into the swimming pool. A whirling belly flop right in front of the girls.

Did they merely step out from the door—whatever that wide opening on the side of the airplane is called—with carefree adolescent freedom? At what point did solid fear turn into limp abandon?

He'd need a cigarette before jumping. It's unlikely they let you smoke on the airplane. But, it might, after all, be his last one. Maybe the stoney sky-jump instructor smokes marijuana up in the cockpit with the pilot? Maybe at five-thousand feet with parachute pack the size of a football he'd take up smoking pot.

He flicked the ceiling light switch. Remembered it did

not work. He walked over to the kitchen table. No need for a night-light. He could see about by the relentless street lamp pestering outside. The brochure was still there, next to the cigarette-filled empty beer bottle. He contemplated an ashtray. In its place, a dirty dinner plate would serve.

Russell opened the brochure, read on the back where the phone number was, where the web address was listed above it: freefallingfun.com. The f's sticking up like gaff-hooks. Free, as in, untethered; not as in cost-less. The ridiculous exorbitant price was spared by tiny italics. "Sky-high," Russell amused. The streetlight dazzled the glossed brochure, making it appear more merry and frivolous. It said the jumps could be booked online. "Put Skydiving on Your Bucket List!" Now there's a tongue in cheek suggestion. Teased with death's choices, Russell lit a cigarette. Everyone featured in the brochure was pictured alive and joyful, more so the plummeting ones, doing that careless fun thing. Clearly, death was a proposal absent on the excitement driven agenda of the gregarious. Anyway, without an Internet connection here in this apartment, anything he wanted to sign-up for would have to be done on a computer somewhere else.

He'd done that—sign up. In the library. At a time prior to the commencement of plaintiff-wife sessions, reproved from home, reproved from his home computer,

Russell had completed a Single's Date-Line profile in a library cubical. Ignoring the adjacent idiot gaming teenagers clustered around the monitors next to him, he determinedly clicked boxes which fit him, faking and fibbing his way suitably through the Man-for-Woman site until the part, "What do you do for fun" appeared. Damn, that's a good question. Back then he hadn't seen the brochure or known anything about skydiving. Even during the puzzling days of Separation Contingency, he wouldn't have considered skydiving as something to do in his new free time. Golf? He didn't know wedge from whiff. He knew clubhouse. "Long walks on beach?" Boring. To and from, from and to, the water splashing on the left, when he turned to go back, was splashing the same way the right. His irritating sandal-shuffling became (prophetically now) the source of "come on, you don't want to lag along by yourself do you" from bare-footed, stone-skipping, Molly, so far ahead. Takes walks on beach? Nope, not me, he sighed. What he really wanted to see was this box: Reckless. Or, at least what he'd expected then.

Stumped unimaginatively in the cubical, all he could think to check under Fun was "Hiking." Yep, walkin' around with a stick. Lookin' at natural stuff. Confidently, he checked Likes-To-Hike from the options boxes, calculating that merely walking around with a staff was vague enough to declare as truthful hiking. And, sure, it was possible he'd do something like that. He cropped five years—no, he changed his mind. Make that eight—off his age. He paused, studied boxes, and then unabashedly checked "Fit", not pouchy. There wasn't a box for Pouchy. He declared "Brown" hair instead of grubby russet because of the same boxless choice. He'd saved choosing an Occupation for last, selecting "I'll Tell You Later."

Encouraged at the end, but viewing it dubiously, he noted that a few women—gals?—had listed their e-mail address. He copied three on a piece of scrap paper he'd found under the monitor: "luvfun4two"; "UBfine4me2"; and "realcreemluvN", which much later, he'd scratched out with a sooty match stick. The paper with the other two names was unfolded on the kitchen table.

Standing there in the hazy florescent kitchen, closing the brochure, he realized what he actually wished for now was wild, vicarious fun. You know, as in Good Ol' Boy Fun—like buzzing stoned and convertibled, driving cross-country. He saw himself with James Dean at the wheel, Bogart riding shotgun, Elvis on guitar, him in the back with Marilyn. Stopping for drinks, like in the painting. Or, zooming around on a motorcycle. Jumping the canyon, like that nutty Kneivel fella, leaping across the great big canyon on an itty-bitty dirt bike.

The Devil Hates a Coward

Maybe even skydiving? Do it with UBfine4me2. Or, luvfun4two. Yep, something like that with them.

A wisecracker voice sneered as if someone was outside the window, "Yeah, right! He conceded to it, matured to the adult actuality of it—frolicking childishly with what's-their-names. Glumly, he tucked the brochure into his boxer's elastic.

The Molly-at-the-beach scene replayed, but in a different setting. In it she is hang gliding behind a speed boat. From inside the binoculars Russell saw his wife with a fantastic smile as wide as the ocean over which she sailed.

Russell patted the tabletop, found the scrap paper, rumpled it, dropped it onto the dinner plate, found the pack of cigarettes. He tapped one forward. He never had to pay attention, especially in darkness, as to which end of the filter-less end to light. He lighted it, a sulfur spark. He exhaled toward the window. The window had an outward breeze. He looked at the paper crumpled between the cigarette butts.

As smoke floated, Russell reconsidered. Yes sir, he'd post them an e-mail. He'd say he was interested in doing it, that he wanted to make a date. No, no, not with luvfun4two. A date for all three of them. A date with Huck and Molly. "Sure enough," he whispered smokily. He'd schedule skydiving online. Yep, he'd message Molly and

Sky Diving

Huck from the library. Tell them he'd booked a dive where they all could jump together? Molly hadn't stopped thrilling about the hang glide all that week. Harold had gone on the roller coaster twice, hadn't he?

Skydiving. It was a precarious idea, wasn't it? But with the notion also came a giddy surprise, it might just actually work. One last get together. It could be like the backyard cookouts of an earlier, compensating time, when Harold brought the beer, and Molly turned up the music, and Russell got out the card table. They'd be a frolicsome threesome imitating the brochure photo, three pair of windstorm hands holding tight, six arms around each other selflessly, six V-shaped legs fluttering merrily, like the triangles of a snowflake, unmindful of the two-hundred mile an hour currents wilding around them.

Wait a minute. He laid the cigarette on the dinner plate. Russell couldn't figure out where all this was coming from. He pulled the brochure out of his boxers. What the hell?

There they were, those ecstatic fallers, portrayed delightfully in the brochure. Could that be them, Molly-Harold-him? In one hand he'd have Molly's; Molly's hand in Huck's—Harold's—him reaching out at four-thousand feet for his, Russell's. He searched the image. Russell pictured Molly, Harold too, looking receptively into his eyes with reciprocal delight, a collective understanding of the impending. During the falling, they'd be happy together, unconscious of the space around them, oblivious to the ground coming up from below.

No, no, no. Russell shook his head and wiped his hair as if something had fallen into it. It couldn't be like that. Not possible. Well, not impossible. It'd be worth a try, if only for a few moments; just to learn how to figure out where they were all supposed to be, to make the triangular snowflake work. They'd have to get oriented quickly, not much time to guess what they were going to do next. Soaring positions; not just tumbling. Taking in the turns and twists as the horrendous winds tried to bluster them apart. Russell didn't know how long he'd have to hold hands, not letting go, so that he wouldn't break the triangle.

Which, after a while he knew he'd have to, of course, release himself; from Harold and Molly, and not just because he was supposed to, not because the ground was soon coming, but because then he'd feel like it. Feel like losing all hands.

The time would have to come certainly. Their V-shaped legs would drift, the triangle sides divide. Russell wondered how he'd feel separated, anxiously watching Molly and Harold—would he no longer be Huck?—fall together, acknowledging that their tumbling might not be as much of hazardous decent as it looked.

He'd raise his hands away, then soar off alone, unattached, arms-free, enjoying his newfound bliss—and yes, fun. He'd probably have a ball!

He folded the brochure, sat on a chair, and considered what kind of pleasure that would be, the flying fall. He tapped his cigarette, the ash near the end.

It'd be short, it wouldn't take long; it says it's about ten minutes. But just before the hard ground came rushing up, he'd glance their way, watch them to see how they'd fade into the clouds, drifting vaporously, like the way the breeze was blowing his cigarette smoke through the kitchen window making like something unseen was carrying it away.

The Adja N'Gor Torch Light

She says Reginettella. I call her Regee Nutella. She calls me Pierre-Figs because she says I am the color of them. She says that I am a man that nourishes. When you say it, her name that is—the one the others the use for her—it rhymes with the pale flowers which stand high at the front of the window of her bedroom. Her skin is of the same color. When she walks, she is tall like them, and when she stretches in the morning and spreads herself, and raises her arms with the yoga, she is like them: a bright white blossom opening in the morning sun.

I can tell you that I call her Regee Nutella. It is the name I have for her because she likes the taste of it, the chocolate spread that is. And because it is quick for me to say.

She has been here momentarily. Now only these seven months. I have been in this place all my life, now thirty-two years. All was always the same until Reginettella came to this place. She is the first woman here. I should say that she is the first woman with skin not like ours. Like mine. I have been pleased that she has been here in this place.

All was always the same until Reginettella came to this place. She is the first woman here. I should say that she is the first woman with skin not like ours. Like mine. I have been pleased that she has been here in this place. And, I will tell also you, I am satisfied that it is her.

Her house is the one room place behind the town; but not at all there by herself. Yes, it is small quarters, and she says that is it just fine for her needs. It is at the back of the bicycle shed so that many cannot see what she does. I know that she is safe. Reginettella. I say her whole name when I speak of her to the others. However, as I've said, I can call her Regee Nutella, alone. Mostly, just Regee. When we are just the two of us.

She does not have a bicycle. She can use one from the bicycle shop. Doumbia is pleased to let her take it. Although she cannot ride any distance. In the day it is hot and the road is harsh. She does not ride during the night. Doumbia will not permit it. He does not work at his shop of the night. She takes her evening meals with Aliou Gueye, and sometimes with Adja Niang. Then it is late.

I bring her the breakfast. The flat bread, and the omelet from my mother. My mother says, "Say that I have no mayonnaise now." My mother never does have the mayonnaise but Reginettella knows that and says, "Tell your mother that the omelet is fine without the mayonnaise." Regee buys the Nutella from Djibril N'diaeye when Djibril has the French bread.

She enjoys to be there in her bedroom of the night; when it is dark, and it is late-night. The night at this time comes soon. She is satisfied to spend the evenings in her room; after I have been there and before I leave her there.

I can spend time in her bedroom. But not alone. Regee wants to be there with me when I am. She says that if some mischief happens, she can say all was fine because she was there with me. But there has been no mischief. Doumbia is at his shop of the day, but often he sleeps inside his shop of the night.

I cannot be there after she has gone to sleep. She likes the bedroom darkened and the rusty spools rolled down, closing the windows so that the louvers shut the strong African air out, and keeps the seal against the things that can crawl through the cracks, and to mute the red crickets that complain too rowdily outside.

I can be there in the morning. I am there when she awakes but not until I see the door has been opened. It is then that I can crank the window spool up and let the bright Africa dawn burst in like glorious trumpet flowers, shining through the slats, and onto her as she stretches with her Yoga.

I can be in her bedroom for a moment during the day.

When it is late during the heat, when she rests on the lounge under the shade tree, then is when I am allowed. I can be there to sweep her floor from the powder that sifts in from the blowing.

I am not allowed into the bedroom after the sun has gone down, and not until after Regee has had the night meal with Adja Niang, and she has returned to her quarters where she will wait until I am there to rattle the louvers closed. I am there after the Atia tea and prayer.

I cannot be in the bedroom as she bathes. I can only fill the steel tub in the corner with the heated water—just to the mark below the rim, too much will spill from her in it. She dips into it alone, foot-stepping wordless. Her silence as she slides makes me think of her legs are like threaded wicks, dipping into wax.

I am not permitted to chose for her the imported bottles of pink salts, yellow oils, amber soaps, orange sponges, or to light the candle that she floats at her shoulders, the ginger-colored flickering as though the glimmer of the oil lamp's taper. Or, be there to hand to her the special red towel. The thick, heavy one that Aliou Gueye washes solely, without any others. I cannot be present as Regee steps from the tub to dry and as she faces the polished flat steel with its buffed shine that I had mounted against the wall for her reflection. She must be alone when she rubs

Torch Light

with the towel, which she does as if doing so is to extinguish the hot wet spices from her shoulders, and her back. And hips. I am told to wait until she bends to towel the last dampness down the back of her legs. She must be by herself when she drapes the red towel as if a djubbeh and stands at the mirror and brushes her hair as the oil light fades.

I am not permitted in her bedroom when she chooses her clothing—those lacey and doily and sleepy clothes from the chest of dressing drawers. It is the thing I made for her—that dresser chest—from the fruit crates, banana boxes, and the ration cartons. I cannot decide the blouse she will choose; the delicate one, as fine as that of compress gauze. I do not fit her feet into the slippers with the thong straps which she draws orderly between each toe.

I am not allowed into her bedroom when she takes her leather journal down from the rough-wood shelf. The shelf where she keeps the sleek Baobab sculpture and the tiny shells from the sandy coast, and the whittled feathery bird carvings that she said were like those from The Gambia, and the ivory figure confiscated from the poachers that I am not to speak about. I am not at hand when she opens the book's leather jacket and whispers some secret message across the pages with her gold pen—the one from the Premier; the one that had signed the truce. I am told not to be there when she closes the journal, and stows the pen in it inside the box. The box of rings and the ropes of pearls and earrings—the ones that look like tiny candelabras. I do not see her latch the brass clasp at the top of the box with its triangle clutch, and she how she slides it underneath the wicker and the quilt of the bed. I am not allowed turning the ivory knob that dims the lantern flame that turns her day to night when she has finished with it. The journal and the day.

I am not allowed into her room until after all of those things have been finished and closed. It will be after I have lowered the awnings and the room has darkened, and she has slipped beneath her blankets that it will be the time for me to come into her bedroom. She will call for me, saying that I can come in now and to bring the Adja N'Gor torch light.

I will press my thumb to the latch of the door handle and gently spin the narrow bolt and softly sweep the door away and slip quietly into her room. I will watchfully point the torch beam to shine across the top of her bed, and not into her eyes, although they will be closed. She lays on her back, her hair tied as if a long burka; the bedsheets under her arms and folded as if a spirit. She opens her eyes when I am near, and she says that I can shine the lamp beam high beyond her, onto the wall above from which hang her personal photographs. I place the light upon each one, especially.

The one of her father, dead now ten years. Him long in Ireland, and not of him dead, but pictured alive and fully haired, and brightly smiled. Not the imagined picture of her father crumpled drunk on the pub floor. I shine upon the photograph of her mother, very alive in South Carolina, bronzed and delightful with large sunglasses, and showing the golf clubs.

Below those are the pictures with Reginettella—Regee—in the frame; the one as she leans against the airplane that sprayed the rice fields that were festered with the locusts. And another: the picture of her in the jeep, the wheels buried into the sloppy mud when she delivered the boxes to Sierra Leone—her long arms resting on the fenders, tan from dirt and sun. The light will reflect off the brass award, the one from the President, the one who had come here.

And the large photo which is my particular favorite of my Regee Nutella—the one that makes like a movie theater poster—of her at this time now fifteen years of the past. She stands at the center stage dressed in a chalk-white gown as willowy and slender as vineyard ivy, her face is an explosion of joy, her lips like red ribbons, and a smile to span an ocean, as she receives that golden award—a shimmering goblet—for all her actress talents.

It is at that time I point the torch away and turn it down and let it dim, and allow the shadows to come intently, and the darkness soften so that she can listen for when her nighttime audience arrives. It is then that I will try to lead her into sleep, to applaud for her softly, and to raise the curtains, and usher in her nighttime chorus of dreams.

You Do Not Think About Your Kaleidoscope

There was a time when you were outward and visible. Had you actually been a beetle or a pigeon or a cloud (and every now and then, perhaps an airplane) they wouldn't have paid any attention; them being such ordinary things. But you liked being those things because they were ordinary—out there out in the backyard. Or, up in the sky. A beetle, airplane, pigeon, and for a time, a hairbrush were common. Ordinary was a good disguise. You did not have in mind an uncommon thing. There were so many those days. They would have been too detectable. You did not decline the desire to become a cloud either; the floating summoned memories. It was when you became the commonplace thing that they watched you. You do not like being outward and visible. The observing.

You did like to avert them. Your mother typically; and in particular, Aunt Marty. You'd jump from the porch, dash into the high grasses in the wheaty meadows behind the house with a desire to be unseen. Of course, they knew what you were up to, or they thought they did; like the beginning of a Chinese checkers game. You chose the yellow marbles. Nevertheless, your mother always conceded to that. You liked it that way; them thinking they knew your reasons. It was your favorite game, the secret plan of the marbles.

Yes, but of course, there were the grasses. At any chance, away you'd run to the tall rows that waited. Quickly, eagerly you'd slip between them with a secretive purpose. That was your favorite thing to do. The disappearing. You'd wait for summer. They said how patient you were. In the spring, before the summer's growing, you'd sit out there on the porch and stare at the stubby blades, not minding that Aunt Marty often said it was like watching grass grow, when she'd done something that bored her. Then school ended and summer started and the furrows filled, and the green-gold shoots talled and the rows matured into corridor-like passages. It was when they were like that when you ran most often. You'd look to see that no one was behind the door—your mother not looking through the screen, Aunt Marty not minding the field—and out you went. The silky fronds were slippery scarves. The hush of grasses made a harmonic swoosh. The cushiony soil, a soft mattress.

You do not know whether your mother fully understood why you were the way you were. You liked it that way. But, at the same time, you wanted her to know. You did not say that you did not want a full knowingness between you. You felt that the two of you had unspokenness. At least in a manner you thought how your mother might describe it to Aunt Marty. You felt connected when asked about how things were, but at the same time do not want to be so thoroughly linked. Like when she'd bought you something and insisted so earnestly that you'd like it. You did, and showed that you did, but at the same time, you do not want what you like to be so visible. You needed remoteness. Although, it did make you happy when she asked because when she did, she'd say that you were special. Caringly she'd tell you she knew you were just pretending and tell you it was okay that you did and that she thought she understood it, just like letting you pick the yellow ones. The pretending.

While you were gone, your mother would go to the kitchen door, and searching through the screen she would see that you were not on the porch. She would scan the field, watching expectantly for the curious waves in the tall grass. Even if Aunt Marty was there sitting at her usual place at the table, she'd exclaim, "Darleen, you got an extraordinary child there." Do you know that your mother always nodded? She'd cup her hands into imaginary binoculars while she'd look for the curious signs of waves in the tall grasses as if a sea captain. Then she'd click the door closed and sit with Aunt Marty. They'd talk about you. Sisters sympathizing about children. You'd be the only child they could talk about; Aunt Marty had a child that did not live. If not about that, they'd talk about the shopping plaza being built down the road. The impending.

Because you were smaller, the grasses were taller. They couldn't see the way you'd run with your arms stretched out that way. You'd be an airplane, fingers for propellers. Or, a cloud, the fields grass an airplane flying through you. When she'd say that she'd guessed what you'd been imagining, thinking that maybe she got it, you'd tell her something misleading instead when she did. No, you'd say, saying that wasn't it. Then you would not imagine the grass reeds as long hair, or a beard and change your imagination as if she'd known it. You did not say that you were a comb, brushing through the field. Or, if she'd actually guessed what you'd been, in its place you'd say you'd been a water beetle. One on a green pond, scurrying and diving. Sometimes, you'd feel like being nothing at all. Go out

About Your Kaleidoscope

there barefoot and just let the delicate tassels at your face and the soft earth between your toes be what they were: tassels and earth. That's all you wanted to feel. When your mother or aunt asked about your feelings, you'd explain them; you'd do it in a way that would make sense to them at that moment. It was usually your mother, or occasionally your Aunt Marty, who'd say, "I see how you are." But, how did they see how you were? The feelings.

Too often, Aunt Marty would call and ask about you. You didn't it ring but from the phone speaker hear Aunt Marty imposing shriek from the *Darleen* at your mother, who held the phone midair and would answer loudly as if she were out of the room. Aunt Marty's imposing voice like that of aluminum foil being pried off the roll. Of course you knew where you were—right there in the same room. You'd eavesdrop and watch your mother talk. Those were the days when Aunt Marty always wanted to know how things were. "Everything all right?" in that boisterous voice she used.

You do not forget easily those days when Aunt Marty would drive to your house and you knew that you would have to stay with her while your mother borrowed the car and drove away. You think it was on Saturdays. She would take her purse and coat, slide courteously behind the wheel, placing her purse alongside, all the while keeping her coat in a neat fold so that it would not rumple, and when settled, she would peer through the windshield while jiggling the keys she would wiggle two fingers, and mouthing *goodbye* would start the car. You recall the way she would yank the gearshift, the way the car shuttered, the lonesome sound the gravel made as she backed away.

While she was gone, Aunt Marty would watch you very much and call to you too often. She wanted to know you were near. She liked to hug and hold. Her big breasts felt spongy to you, as if her large bra were holding back something waterlogged. You did not separate the smell of the body talcum she used from the scent of your mother's laundry powder. You could not have been more inflexible if you had been a plaster statue.

Aunt Marty always asked about what you were doing. "What're you being?" she'd insist far too inquisitively. She would bring coloring books with pictures of nature scenery, or circus animals, or famous presidential monuments, and get out your crayons and colored pencils. You would shade in just a little place on the page—the pedestal the elephant stood on; one or two cacti in the desert; the clown's hat—and when she was in the livingroom resting, you'd set it all aside and go out to the porch to await your mother's return. The predicting.

While you did, Aunt Marty would come to the door and spy through it. "There you are," she'd say when she saw that you were there. So obvious, wasn't it? That you were. She'd tap at the screen. "You silly thing. Just sitting out here alone, uh? Don't you want something to do?" She'd glance at the field. "Other than that." You did not want to know if Aunt Marty thought you would do what you were thinking of doing.

She'd scratch at the door screening as if it were your coloring book. "You didn't finish coloring. You left the elephant undone. It's supposed to be all grey. Not just some. The clown hat shouldn't be black." She'd open the door ajar. "You seem sad." She'd close the door, go inside. "Your mother will be back soon." You did not bother that Aunt Marty worried unnecessarily about you. You did not know she often was uneasy about the tending she had to do when your mother was gone. Immediately upon her departure, Aunt Marty would begin inquiring about your condition. Each time you'd pass through the kitchen she'd catch you. "How're you feeling?"

You'd say *okay*. Then you'd look out at the grassy meadow, the longing tassels, the rows of secrets. The longing.

You did not want to be uncooperative. To show that you were not sad, or how you were not longing the way she might have thought, you said *I'm just being quiet.* You did not like that she'd look out at the field, down at you, and then back at the field, but she'd pull the screen door closed, then go away. "I see," she'd say worriedly. As soon as the door snapped shut, you'd leap off the porch and run out into the field.

After a while, because she'd sensed you were gone, she'd go back to the door. She'd tilt alertly through the opening, askew half inside and half outside, cocking her head sideways the way a dog listens for something it can't see, but might have heard. You do not like to picture Aunt Marty as a dog, but when she'd make her head like that—the teapot to boil; the phone to ring; the car to arrive—for a just a minute you did not think it was inconsiderate to picture it.

When you got back she'd still be standing behind the door, tapping at the screening. She'd announce mockingly, as if to another person who'd also been waiting, "finally." She'd clap, the applauding made the screen cloth wiggle. The wiggle made it look like some other person behind the door was standing there in a grayed smoky haze, not Aunt Marty. "I was looking for you," the misty person would say. When the door opened, the haze cleared and real Aunt Marty appeared. "Did you get lost?" You said no, that you knew where you were. Hands raised, Aunt Marty begged sarcastically, "Where was that?" You said you'd been shopping. The field rows like store aisles; the sky above, florescent lighting. You raised your hands as she had, and said that you didn't buy anything. That's why you didn't anything with you. You showed her your hands, then sat on the porch. Aunt Marty pointed at the meadow. "I don't know what all the attraction is about."

Or, at other times, she'd ponder to herself aloud, so that you heard it, and say she was confused about your feelings. About what it was you were being. And why that was. You said you thought people shouldn't wonder about what you were feeling or being or anything; that you thought they could just tell by the way you were just being. But you did not say whether it was an airplane, or a comb, or a beetle or a cat—or nothing at all. Instead, you went upstairs. On the way, Aunt Marty said, "Your mother understands you better than me. When she gets home you can tell *her* what you've been doing." You did not brood over not telling Aunt Marty what you'd done. Which, she did—ask you—just before your mother came home.

While in your room, you heard a car drive up to the house—your mother returning. By the time you arrived downstairs, she was standing in the kitchen, her coat hanging loosely over her forearm. It looked like it was folded in the same way she had made it while getting into the car before she had driven away. Between her other arm and her chest, she clutched her purse closely, as if she had not driven herself to the house but, instead, had gotten off a bus. She gave you a full-sized smile like she had been gone a very long time and was surprised at how big you had grown. "There you are!" She set her coat over a chair, opened her purse, and from it, held a small package. "I know you'll like this," announcing it in the sense someone with a souvenir from that far away place they had been would. "Look," handing it to you on her palm like a tray "You'll see."

Whenever your mother would leave the house for the day, there would always be a present for you when she returned. You would pretend the gift was unexpected. Your mother acknowledged the ruse, twinkling, "What were you expecting?" It was what you two did then, like choosing the Chinese Checker's marble—you always took yellow. You did not speculate that your gift was an apology for her being gone, or a reward for you being there when she got back. It was merely an anticipated ploy; the trick of the game. "What did you expect?" she would ask knowingly.

Nothing is what you would not say. Because each time it was something, and often, bewildering. Like getting that paddle with a picture of a hippopotamus with a hole in the center of the hippopotamus' wide-opened mouth that

About Your Kaleidoscope

you were supposed to get a ball attached to a bouncy string through. It didn't. Eventually, the string stretched, snapped, and the ball disappeared. The hippopotamus paddle went lost somewhere; missing in an unknown place, its large mouth still expecting a ball. Once, it was a pack of trick cards. Aunt Marty suggested, "So now you can perform magic," encouragingly. A subtle difference in the constellation of hexagons on the back of the cards revealed— only to the magician, you—what was on the front.

There was the day your mother gave you a kaleidoscope. It was a wonderful thing; a twisting mirage. Through it, all was tinted mysteriously: wedge-shaped oddities; triangular weaving; broken shapes, as if a shattered stained glass window. It was scary at first, the real world broken up into a confounding puzzle, but after you got used to it, twisting it round and round, the distorted images began to appear comfortable.

You did not feel like saying when our mother put her hand on your head and asked what you'd been doing. But, what you said was that you'd been doing nothing. You wanted it to sound indifferent, in the same way you'd say it to Aunt Marty whenever you were handed the phone. You thought *nothing* was a good answer for then.

You did not feel offended by Aunt Marty's puzzled look. You did dislike that she insisted, twisting her head as if she were peeking at you through your kaleidoscope. To you, she was doing the dog listening thing, ears up. "Did you go running?" You did not choose untruthfulness. *Yes, of course* you said, adding while looking at her, that, no, that there wasn't a good reason. That it was just nothing.

At which your mother inquired expectantly, rehearsed, as if asking for a clue to a riddle she'd solved once before. "So, you just run just run for no reason?" Before you spoke, she turned to Aunty Marty who stood aside, waiting vigilantly until relieved of her watch. She shrugged absently at Aunt Marty and whispered obviously. "It's nothing," petitioning Aunt Marty in a way that seemed as if she was searching for the same riddle. Your mother blinked slowly, awkwardly, as if her eyelids were squeezing something spongy. You did not want them to be tears.

Each time she asked about your feelings, about what you were being, if you were lonesome, if you'd like a playmate, you said *of course not,* and said that it was just feeling like being something that you liked. You do not want a playmate. The being something else is just part of your feelings. But they thought it was more, that they— your mother, Aunt Marty, those people they do not name—could see that you had a good imagination. Your mother would say to Aunt Marty, "running between the field rows is simply her imagining." Yes, you had a good

About Your Kaleidoscope

imagination then. Your mother and Marty said they knew it when you were. At least that's how they made it sound, that they knew. You did not feel then that they knew it wholly, understandably. They'd say it when they'd seen that you'd come back from it. They couldn't know all that they said they saw. All they could see was the field, a tall row of swaying grass, some unseen thing streaming through it. What you did not like was them wanting to know what it was—making you so outward and visible. The uncomfortableness.

These days you do not reflect uncomfortably about being outward and visible. Nowadays, especially today, you do not stop considering being inward and invisible. You can recall being imaginative, insecurely. That's the way it is now. Most days, you rarely deliberate that your mother does not forget you were an imaginative child. When prompted by something you do now it does not take much to spell her memory of it. Not the just way she'd noticed the things the way you do now , but she also remembers the days when you lived out by the grass fields. Back when they were still there. These days her memories are covered with curvy streets and tedious houses and shopping centers as dull and flat as cardboard. You live far away from that country, inside the city. In an apartment, alone. Without your mother. Upstairs. Behind a door.

Today you're nervous. You're waiting behind the door until the postman comes, in the way you'd wait for a telephone call, but wouldn't answer it when it rang. The postman, actually a postwoman, even in this neighborhood, needs to get there and leave. You'll wait for all the other apartment mail to be delivered. It's not that you need yours. It's not the mail that keeps you behind the door. You say, "All I want is to have her distribute the mail, finish up, and leave." Simple. You just want to go outside and get on the bus, unnoticed.

You do not go out; you emerge. So that when you do, you want your intention concealed. You think a gecko's camouflage is not a terrible . Today you want a clandestine plan. Today you have planned a daunting trip to the Glenwood Shopping plaza. You have to take the bus. The Glenwood #67 and ride it all the way to the end of the Glenwood Road. Not too complicated a trip for you. It's just one bus out to Glenwood, but probably too much Glenwood for one day.

At last, the downstairs door thumps open and the mailwoman comes into the foyer. She clumps letters into the metal boxes. The big families get glossy thick catalogues and large puffy packages. Others get that too, but

About Your Kaleidoscope

also get broad pamphlets and long envelopes. Even Mrs. Schpeidreck gets volumes of mail. Noisy mail. When the postwoman drops the neighbor's mail, it sounds like apples falling into empty buckets.

Your mail is noiseless. That's good. You do not believe your mailbox is the same size as the big family mailboxes. But heavy, big mail doesn't arrive inside yours. It is light, small mail that flutters into the box. Usually, it stays in there for a while before you get the courage to check it. It rests in its box for a few days and you do not bother with it, as if a bird had nested and shouldn't be disturbed. One day you looked inside and saw four blue-speckled eggs. You left them alone until the eggs hatched and the fledglings flew away.

At times your mail is like venomous snakes, full of terror and anguish, a thing to avoid, something that bit you. You do not suffer abstinence from avoiding the mail, because on a susceptible day, misery can begin with seeing hazardous mail. You do not like to recall those gas company bills, and the checks you wrote that were returned, *Insufficient Funds*. Inside the mailbox, those threatening envelopes hammered loudly at twenty dollars a whack.

Opening and closing doors shows impatience. You do not like that it shows, so you stop doing it and wait. It will not be much longer until Mrs. Schpeidreck comes out of her apartment to get her mail. Or, as you like to say, "Leap and snatch." You do not like her scrawny legs, her long arms, her piercing eyes; her curved jaw. She is short. Her legs, her wing-like arms, brings an insect to mind. You do not like being in front of her door when it opens, her apartment emits the odor of spoiled bananas. Mrs. Schpeidreck is a fruit spider; she attacks her mailbox, snapping at it as if there were insects trapped inside.

Keep your ear to the door so you can hear what's going on. You whisper a faint plea, *hurry up, give out the mail. Please leave.* You peek, and through the slight gap at the door you'll see that the mailwoman has at last set all the packages down and has ticked all the box doors closed. Now she's opening the foyer door and as she closes it, she walks down the stoop. There, she's turned and is going away. Next, Mrs. Schpeidreck will charge at her mail. Listen. Her door's squeaking. She's coming out. See? There she goes. She's emptied it. Drained, it snapped shut. She's gone back into her apartment, into the breathless trapped air. Now she's pulled the heavy door behind her. Now is your chance to rush downstairs, to go out to the street. Then, get to the bus stop.

You count: *one, two, three...*and more. It is the fat Puerto Rican. His door is across from Mrs. Schpeidreck's. It reminds you of the time he showed you his rude maga-

About Your Kaleidoscope

zines. You were going down stairs, and he stood at his door and stopped you. You did not want to stop there, but be courteous you said *okay*. He said, "Look at this magazine." Instead, you looked into his apartment. He held the magazine open to some pages. Like Mrs. Schpeidreck's his apartment had terrible air. Musty, it smelled like the rusty potato bin your mother had. The curtains hanging around the windows were brown and crumpled; perhaps made from burlap. At the center of the room, a lumpy sofa wilted; a gnawed upholstered dirty thing that slouched in the corner. From a box-cluttered table near the kitchen door, pale rope-like cables reached into other rooms, reminding you unhappily of the spindly roots at the bottom of the potato bin. He showed you a page. On it were vividly naked women. They appeared to be shouting at something, or howling painfully. You hunched, glanced avertedly into his apartment. He saw where you were looking, not at his magazine. He twisted, stood to block his doorway, and snarled. More as if growling, he barked, "What! You snoopy dog. Go mind you own stinky business, you nosey dog." You ran upstairs, pushed a chair against the door. That was an example of an awful day.

At last, Mrs. Schpeidreck's door clicks. Hurry, grab your backpack. Run down the stairs. Not that fast; it's like you're plunging, not footstepping. Watch the stairtreads.

You almost slipped once hurrying like that. You will not make eye contact if that man is there. If Mrs. Schpeidreck peeks out, ignore her too.

You made it past the apartments; now open the foyer door and go outside.

Good. See? Not many clouds. Mostly sun. Checking the street, you stand awhile—there's time. *No one here.* The Glenwood # 67 will be here soon. You adjust your backpack. You ask, *are the coupons in it?*

Richie stands inside the fence over there in the far corner. He faces east; where the sun shines between the buildings. He holds the iron pickets firmly. You think you understand why he does not like the other corner, where the fence joins the building closely, where it's shadowy during the day. Now he moves out of the corner, toward you. You know why he moves that way, but you are not aware that others do not. He sways back and forth, doing that rocking thing he does at this time of the day— especially when it's sunny. After a while he will move farther, beyond the corner, but always rocking, rocking. He will feel his way along the picket tips, watching the sun, waiting for three o'clock. You are not unaccustomed to the way he does that. You do not need to watch the way he moves along the length of the fence, thrumming the pick-

About Your Kaleidoscope

ets, sensing them with his tiny fingers, passing over the ones with sharp points.

You are not troubled about not knowing how old he is. He seems to be fixed in time, so you have made him a young boy. Also, you have considered it likely he could be much older. It is difficult, because he seems to have stayed only as tall as the fence during all these days. He does not notice it.

Now you walk toward him. He won't see you from there. Why is it that nobody gets a pair of those dark glasses for him? His father certainly will not. Instead, Richie is left to squint which makes him look merely disabled. You say that people with Richie's kind of mentality always look befuddled, and in another manner, enlightened about something. He seems ageless, like a youngster and an old man simultaneously.

Probably, Richie's father is working on one of the apartments somewhere. Like trying to fix something he should have done months ago. Like the outlet in your kitchen—the one that sparks when anything's plugged into it. There was a time when you wanted to ask Richie why his father leaves him out here inside the fence all day, and if he knew, does he mind it that he does. I know you haven't asked yet. You've assumed that Richie probably wouldn't even understand the question. Instead, you've just passed by and not asked him any questions. You also sensed his place. That's an empathy I've recognized in you lately. Imagining yourself as Richie, you wouldn't want to be answering at lot about why you were, either. You avoid questions about why things are the way they are, or suppose the reasons they are. You are not inclined to answer them, and there are those you do not like to ask--the ones that you wished would not be answered. The asking makes you think you'll sound like your mother. Reasons—explanations—as you've said, are insensible. The grasses were tall. That wasn't always the reason for running in them.

Ritchie's turning your way and is gradually working his way toward you. See how he clenches the fence balusters as if handles. Yes, like gear teeth, now that you say it. His head is turned upward, his face into the sun, as he always does when it's sunny, even today, although there are a few clouds. The way that he is right now, if you duck slightly and move slowly, you might be able to sneak under him. But if he notices you're there, he'll try to reach through the fence and touch you.

Good. You made it. He didn't see you. At least not in the way he does. Had you made a shadow, he'd have searched the obscurity recklessly like an overturned mole caught in daylight.

About Your Kaleidoscope

The bus won't come for a while. Sit down on that bench. You can still watch for the bus there. Watch Richie. Now his head is cocked in your direction. Do you think he's sensed you passed him? It's curious the way he follows the sun, unless, like you, someone knows why. You've said how he's just like a sundial; a clockwork pun. See, even in the short time you've been here, he's moved forward a few pickets. He wags his head at the sunshine, bobbing up and down rhythmically. You allow that the sun beating down on his face has a tempo perhaps only Richie can feel. You've felt it too, flat on your back, looking up through the canyon of wheat grass into the high sun against a light-blue sky the color of bright crêpe' paper. He squints at the sun, like you often did, and you think that maybe the sunlight through his eyelids makes him happy. Like that silly song your Aunt Marty used to sing. Something about sunflowers and how they're happy to follow the sun. As if she would've known a happy sunflower from an unhappy one.

Some people are coming. Do you think Richie will let them pass without reaching out? You know that when they get right alongside Ritchie, he'll ask them if it's going to rain. "Gonna rain? Gonna rain? Gonna rain?" Or, if not that, his other thing, "Three o'clock? Three o'clock? Three o'clock?"

The Devil Hates a Coward

They've stopped at the fence. They must know him. Do you know them? Are they from this neighborhood? No, you do not have to look. The tall woman is telling Richie, "No, Richie. It's not going to rain. No rain today." The other woman says, "No, not yet, Richie. It's not three o'clock yet." The man pats Richie on the head and then looks at the sky, "No rain." They all leave him. They seem happy that they've made him happy. Richie still holds onto the fence, turning his head to where he might think they are and calls out to that place, "Three o'clock?", his blindness locked into the brightness between.

What's that? Yes indeed, it doesn't look like rain today. Yet look at Richie, standing there, swaying, drunk-like, head thrown back, bobbing, worried about it raining. You're troubled by Richie. He's an outward, visible person who exists in an inward, invisible place.

You do not tell yourself that saying to Richie that it' not going to rain today won't make any difference to him. So you go over there and tell him that you think it's probably not going to rain today, but come back to the bus stop quickly. You do not want to miss the bus. As you wait, you do think about the time his father forgot about Richie out there in the rain.

It was the day his father was working in one of the apartments, or drinking, or "layin' some pipe," as he once rudely told you. Why did he say that? Do you think he meant Ashley's pipes? That tar-eyed girl who lives above you who you think is a whore because she goes out every night but not during the day. Sometimes there are men who come up the stairs and then go down again after not being there long. A couple of times there were older men and Ashley is not old.

Anyway, as you recall, Richie's father was distracted and did not notice the rainstorm coming. It started around nine in the morning and rained like a broken fire hydrant. You watched from your window. Thunder and scary lightening, too. After about an hour, Richie's father comes dashing out the apartment swearing at Richie, screaming, "You fuckin' idiot. Fuckin' shit. Goddamn. Out here in the fuckin' rain. Jesus Christ. Can't you see its pourin' fuckin' rain?" Richie was sopped—saturated is a better word—like a too-soaked washcloth. His father pulled him out over the pointy fence rails, set him on the wet sidewalk, and went to his truck to get some large trash bags. You do not think: *I know what's going on down there.* The *Richie is there getting so wet, I should go get him.* What was going on down there, the rain and thunder so loud, or what had happened until you heard Richie being carried past your door, sobbing, then upstairs into Ashley's apartment.

The Devil Hates a Coward

Later, Ashley relayed what had happened. You do not know why she would choose to speak to you. Firstly, you avoid talking to her. Secondly, with all of that makeup on her eyes bring a raccoon to mind, and those little silver barbells pierced through her tongue make you queasy. When she speaks her words slither out as if she had been chewing something rubbery, deflated balloons. What Ashley said was that because his father had taken all of Richie's clothes down into the dryer, Richie had to spend the day wearing a trash bag, just his head sticking out, like a black poncho draped over a post. He left Richie in her apartment while he went somewhere. She also said that when she took a shower and got out, Richie was there in the bathroom. She didn't know if he'd done anything disgusting, but the way his legs were sticking out of the bottom of the bag was weird. She said she'd heard that retarded people had big penises—*dick*, was the word she used—to make up for their small brains. Isn't that the way she is, saying things in her weird and off-the-wall way to you, just to see what you might do? Her balloon mouth flapping. Lisping.

After that, you wondered if Richie had ever seen a girl naked before. If Ashley was the first, she wouldn't have been a good impression—all metaled up like a chain. Ashley has small breasts.

About Your Kaleidoscope

And then, weirdly, it happened again about a month later; Richie, out in the rain. You did not know what to do. You did not want to know that Mrs. Schpeidreck finally came, opened the fence gate door, and took him into her apartment. He was just as soaked as the other time. Richie probably had to breathe in her dreadful air. You're unsure whether Mrs. Schpeidreck would have taken a shower with someone in the apartment, but Richie isn't just someone. But you're not certain about either of it.

Richie's father came and got Richie from Mrs. Schpeidreck's apartment. It was close to quitting time anyway; about three o'clock. Richie wore a large, grayed suit, like a baggy old man. Maybe some clothes from her dead husband. On the way down the stairs, Richie began crying, "Gonna rain? Gonna rain?"

Ever since that day, whenever you pass, Richie asks if it's going to rain.

Thinking about whether it will rain or whether it's three o'clock in Richie's world, you get off the bench and begin to walk toward him. You hold your backpack with both hands, tight to your chest. He shakes his head, as if asking if someone is there. When you get closer, he puts his arms around his neck. Perhaps it's the way a blind person senses someone, something, approaching. When you are close, he cries, "Three o'clock? Three o'clock?"

You change your mind. You turn away and go back to the bench. You whisper; more to yourself than for him to hear. *No, Richie, it's not three o'clock. It's ten twenty-eight.*

You do not like his three o'clock thing either. Three o'clock is the time something wakes you up in the night. When you have to go to the bathroom. Even in the afternoon. Three o'clock is always a bad time. It's always too early or too late to do anything.

Here comes the bus. It hisses to a stop, puffs, and the walk-up steps drops. The bus lowers to the street as if bowing. You board and take a seat halfway into the bus, behind the handicapped railing, under the package rack, away from the driver. You don't like sitting on the bench-styled seats; you like the ones that face sideways so you can see the street ahead and behind you. Your seat is orange and smooth and warm. A comfortable one. You're pleased that there were plenty of seats to choose from. Not many ride in the middle of the morning. There's just one other passenger, a thin black woman. She faces forward in an aisle seat, diagonally. She wears oversized sunglasses, making it difficult to know if she's looking at you. She looks like a fly. You fold your backpack in your lap. Check the side pocket, pinch it to ensure that your money pouch is securely deep inside. It's there. Do not take it out. If you take it out and check for the money, someone might notice and

About Your Kaleidoscope

know that you have it. But it's just the black woman and she's just gazing out the window and doesn't seem to be noticing anything but where the bus is going.

You take the advertising booklet out of your pocket. You feel how long, straight and narrow it is. The coupons are loosely fastened, the staples too small to hold so many pages. You feel one of the staple points. It's not sharp; it's dull and bent. You read the booklet's cover and think the words are funny—all of the B letters are large and slanted and say, "BOB BRINDLES BUNDLE OF BARGAINS BARN." They read as if sounded by a stutterer, or if Ashley had said them. You flip through the pages to where the coupons for appliances are. The woman in the huge sunglasses sees what you're doing. She smiles. Maybe there's a shine behind the dark glasses? Richie would look silly in those glasses.

The booklet mentions many other free things you can get with the coupons: a free appointment with a hairdresser; some bar-b-que tongs; a tiny yard ornament shaped like a pair of bouncing rabbits; a large sponge on a stick to wash a car windshield (fashioned like an enormous toothbrush); a buy-one-get-another-free, pizza restaurant offer. There's none of that that's any benefit to you. Your hair is too short; you do not like grilled food; you do not have a car; and you can barely manage one meal—how

The Devil Hates a Coward

could you possibly eat two? Maybe save one for Richie? Having never seen him eat anything, you wonder what food he likes.

The bus turns a corner and stops. A dusty-skinned man with a turban comes aboard. His tan clothing is crisp and unwrinkled, like postal wrapping paper. He takes a seat on the other side of the aisle. He has a large book with a soft linen cover. The title lettering is in the shape of triangles and stars. He winks at you. His eyes are like black olives. His smile, mannerly. Occasional friendliness makes you uncomfortable. You look away, then down at your coupon booklet. While you're reading, he opens his book and what looks like butterflies come out between the pages, their folded wings like golden snowflakes. You do not look at him, but just as you do, he closed the book and the butterflies disappeared inside the linen cover.

You didn't see the butterflies because you were concentrating on the coupons. You want to see more of what's inside the booklet. It shows snap-lid storage containers, assorted screwdrivers, heart-shaped dishtowels, a DVD collection about national parks. You do not own a DVD player and when you think about it, you can't remember the last time you watched a movie at home. Or anywhere.

The bus starts. You wonder about the woman with the sunglasses, where she went, but actually don't care.

About Your Kaleidoscope

You just want a new toaster. At last, toward the last pages, you get to the ones with pictures of appliances. There it is—the toaster you want; a shiny one with white sides, black levers. Probably has a long cord. Brand new. Right out of the box when you get it home.

Small print at the bottom of the page says, "Present in Whole." What do you think that means? Do you think that means the entire booklet? You think it means just show only the coupon itself; not the whole booklet. You turn the page. You are wrong. There on the back in large warning words it says, "VOID IF PAGE IS REMOVED". It's the same sort of letters on signs saying that there can be no swimming without a lifeguard. But the coupon doesn't have the black band across a swimmer. Of course, even if there were a lifeguard, and the water was warm and safe, you wouldn't go anyway; definitely not your favorite wants.

A new toaster is what you want now. The old one is in your closet, broken. It can't be fixed. The bottom is cracked, the metal parts lie scattered, as if bleeding from the slots. You've got a television that used to work in there too, crouched in the dark against the wall like something cornered. Your other TV sits on a wobbly table. You do not watch it because you can't get reception. Even when you twist the antennas, all you see is a fuzzy, woeful picture.

The Devil Hates a Coward

You miss your toast, and those Pop Tarts; the cinnamon ones with chocolate syrup on it. You do not think about the way you miss eating toast the way you like it is peculiar. The thought, not the toast being that way. Your mother saw the way your toaster was before it broke. You do not consider plugging it in again. You hear your mother saying, "Don't even think about plugging that thing in." You like the tea kettle; the one you got for your birthday. And something else? You consider the tea kettle unlike the toaster, differently. You're not certain if it was the cords on those things or if it was the outlet that Richie's father was supposed to fix that made them spark, then fall to the floor. After you told her about it, she said, "You need a new toaster." Then later, she gave you those coupons you have. She said, "Use them before they expire." You do not want them to expire. That's why you're going to use them at this time.

Now, the bus is somewhere along Hazelwood Street, far from where you're going. Your seat is uncomfortable. You change. That one feels just the same; it's slopped and slippery. It occurs to you that maybe you should get off the bus, take another one back home. Do this some other time. The man in the turban watches you shifting between seats. He nods at you. You do not like the way he acts, like he recognizes you are nervous. Something

About Your Kaleidoscope

makes you think he might ask you how you are, simply politely. Not in the manner Aunt Marty would, though. If he does, what will you tell him?

Along the way, there behind a telephone pole, a three-legged boy-dog stands. Will it pee? How? "The bus passes, the dog is unseen. Right now, it's all uncertain. You study where the bus is. You think you are halfway there. Out to where Bob Brindle' Bundles of Bargains s is still much further; out where you and your mother used to live. Where you were younger. Where you ran in the fields. Where it was exciting. Where your imagination was. Your house was one of the few in a place where the town just kind of ended. You and your mother had a small house, but it had large windows. People could see in, but that was all right then. If you looked out some windows and faced one way, there were some houses. When you turned around, you could see the fields. Your mother could walk down the street to the store. And you rode your bike around. There were kids around back then, but you did not do much of the things they did.

You wouldn't ride your bike there now. You don't even have one. The big stores arrived quickly, then just as suddenly, they departed, leaving abandoned hollow shells like snakes shedding skin. New people came to the neighborhood, strange men stood on the corners. Your mother said they were Spanish. You and your mother moved out when they moved in. Because of the deserted buildings, not necessarily because of the people. Yes, of course, they made your mother nervous. Aunt Marty wasn't around anymore.

These days it is impossible for pedestrians and dangerous for bicycles. It's all busy lanes and scary traffic. The sidewalks are neglected and shameful. The plazas, like Indian ruins. That's why you're terribly anxious about going out there, riding here alone on a bus without passengers.

The bus slows, there is someone waving a pair of sticks. The bus stops at a place where here's no wait sign. A woman steps off the curb, then outside at the front of the bus, she taps one stick against the bus. The driver points to the door. He opens it. The steps lower. She walks to them. She looks at them with a tired expression, like they were the stairs to a very high place. She puts a foot on the first tread. She climbs in using her sticks like ski poles. As the driver takes her pass, she leans on the ticket box. Her pass returned, she looks down the bus aisles with weary eyes. Between the aisles, she doesn't ask for help, but they way she is staggering, you sense she could use some. You're afraid to help. Is it those sticks? The man in the turban has his eyes closed; the book of butterflies rests on his lap.

It takes her a long time to hobble between the seats. From his mirror, the bus driver watches her, but not too

About Your Kaleidoscope

long. The bus lurches forward. At the motion, she reaches desperately for a seat to hold. The bus movement knocks her forward. She plunges forward. She crumbles into the seat next to you as if she'd been trampled into it. Her sticks clatter. You adjust your backpack. She turns, looking at you there, she grins, but she does not make you feel pleased that she has. Her chin and forehead have perforations. Something that is hair covers her dark ears. One of her sticks pushes your backpack. Her eyebrows are as if applied with shoe polish. They rise apologetically when she draws the stick away. Again, she grins. But you appraise her smile incongruously because she has remarkably wonderful teeth. Dazzling and luminescent. Too white. The bus whines, turns another corner, and stutters nervously as it accelerates.

The old woman shakes and wiggles. You do not hypothesize diseases, but you do speculate possibility. As the bus pitches, she leans forward, places her head between her legs, arches her back, and presses her hands on her knees. She tucks her sticks under her shoulder and touches her head against the seat ahead of her.

It is a little bit later, some street stops later, after you've moved closer to the window, she's making flapping motions. It did not upset you until she began to speak. It was more of a yelp. She said, "Elbowroom, elbowroom," banging her arms backward against the seat. You tilted away. She brought to mind a bat trapped in a crack trying to fly.

After a moment, she's calm. Pushing ahead on her sticks, she looks around. "More room," she cackles. The bus gears shift. Her face pressed against the window, she peers through it. You believe she might be astray, on the wrong bus. While she looks, focused puzzled in that way, you move away three seats. You hope now she has lots of room.

The bus comes to a traffic light and waits. While it idles, the old woman stretches and then—horrors—she slides over to you, one bench away. She acts like you aren't even there, that you're invisible. She sits up alertly, produces a cigarette and tries to light it. The match does not spark, nor does it connect to the cigarette. The driver snarls, "No smoking on the bus." In one crippled hand she holds the unlighted match in the other, the cigarette. She remains fixed that way until, until after a few blocks, she twists in her seat and puts the match back into her pocket and places the cigarette behind an ear hidden deep into the lair of starched hair. She grins at you, satisfied at the cigarette stashing; her incongruent teeth beam. Through them she mumbles, "Elbowroom."

About Your Kaleidoscope

You nod trivially. You do not know how to be polite to this strange woman. Instead you ignore her with the same manner you do when Richie turns his head toward you, as she has, asking innocently—helplessly—if it will rain, if it's three o'clock. If there's more room.

She, like Richie, gives you uneasy feelings. Both of their troubles seem alike—their powerlessness exposed. You weigh on that likeness; perhaps there's something in them that you might share? You disregard your thought of vulnerability. You don't get it; not even easy things. Like three-legged dogs. Struggling invisibly in an obviously easy world? That kind of thinking gets you upset. You, too, look out the window for something recognizable.

The air inside the bus feels sticky, oily, like an adhesive drying. Stickiness . The air outside the bus looks hot and humid, if you could feel it too. The street macadam glistens wetly. The sunshine is thick and translucent, the air motionless, as if someone had set a plastic dome over the day.

The bus stops at a medical building. The turban man stands, tucks his book under his arm, and gets off. At the bus stop he takes out a large key and unlocks the door of a little office. Now you are alone with the disturbing woman. You do not count the driver. He is a part of the bus.

Once more, the bus stops but no riders come on. You use this as an excuse to go to the front where you can pretend your stop is next. The woman gets up too and follows you. She takes a spot so close that her sticks touch you. While she settles. You watch the driver, not her. You jiggle the little clip that zips the backpack pocket where your coupon booklet hides. Something tugs at the zipper. Two lengthy fingers tap at your backpack pocket. You fear stealing. She leans. She leans too close. Now she takes a backpack strap between her pencil-like fingers, pulls it gently. She sighs. Here she faces you, saying, "Dun hafta gotta now. Maw goo summa'time." You shrink, as if smaller will make you invisible. Now don't you wish you were a beetle, digging a burrow? You consider a pigeon, one that could fly out the window. Then—isn't this just awful—she reaches over, touches your arm, and now she's holding out her other hand, the one not on the backpack strap, making a fist. Will she strike? You cannot fight. She clasps her fingers, like trying to stop something. You take her other hand away from the zipper clasp. She takes a stick with it, rests her hand. You do not want to say *take your other stick in your hand*, so you do nothing. She holds her fist near to you. Her fist unspools. Her creaky fingers spread open, knuckles as bolt hinges. You are alarmed their noiseless-ness. Here, while you are wordless, she asks, "See, pieces?" She looks to see that you have. "Pressed you."

There mounded in the furrowed paw of her hand are what at first appear to be peanuts, still dirty in their shells. Yet, for a moment, candies came into mind. You did not want those candies. You did not want to imagine her to be a witch, but you considered poison. Again, she asks, "Pressed you?" Here is a misunderstood question, and an unanswerable one at that. She releases the held stick with the hand that holds the stick and with another fragile finger, and from that hand she pokes at those collected things there in her palm that she's opened for you to see. Again, her eyes look into yours, pleading. No, you are not going to touch them.

They are not soiled peanuts. Not candy bits. They are nuts and bolts, corroded with a rusty confection. She holds her palm outward, as if to feed them to something. She offers them to you, "Elbowroom pieces. Uh?" You say, *No.* She takes your hand.

Now, because at this complex moment you cannot quickly reason why not to, so you let your hand be taken; reluctantly, limply, submissively. She motions you to open your hand, like she has hers. You do not know why you shouldn't obey. She sprinkles the nuts and bolts onto your palm, and as you mind, she folds your fingers around the

The Devil Hates a Coward

nuts and bolts tightly, just as she had had them before. With her other papery, blue-veined hand she pats your leg. Because you feel as if obliged through a spell, you unclip an accessible backpack pouch and dutifully slide those nuts and bolts into its emptiness. That makes her smile. Her mouth opens broadly, her lips stretch; bright teeth glint. Their inappropriateness, made yet more startling as she clicks them.

You make a smile, too; though not as openly bright as she has made. You maintain your teeth closed. She clothes her mouth, while continuing to observe you

Oh, now you wish more earnestly that the Glenwood bus stop will come. An outward gaze through the window reveals no signpost. No passenger has come aboard.

Is she saying something? You do not reveal that you are not listening. She speaks regardless that you want to pretend to listen. There next to you is someone who you suppose other people only stare at, not listen to. Like Richie behind the fence. One to whom no one would speak if not spoken to first. You are not an initiator of conversation. Although, because you suffer still that spellbound feeling, which, after a few moments, you indeed listen to what she's saying. You do not decline that what the old woman is saying is not like listening to creepy Ashley, or unexplained Mrs. Schpeidreck, or even Richie's thoughtless father, or any of them. You listened to Aunt Marty; at least the middle of it. And, you listen compliantly to Richie. He is easy to understand, he says the same thing over.

Maybe because the bus is not groaning with engine shifting or because the woman is so near to your ear, her words not unambiguous now. Her diction is clearer, like the way the wind swish is silenced when you lay on your back between the tall grasses. You do not glance out the bus window to divert her gaze as she speaks. She says she's been to the petting zoo—to feed the animals. She cups her hands together like a basin. With her thumbs, she strokes at a place inside her bowled hands that you are supposed to see. She says that one of the animals has bitten her there, at a place where her thumb points. You do not reveal that you cannot see any animal bite, but you nod thoughtfully.

Maybe because you do not exhibit recognition, she jerks her hands away, pulls one of her sticks between her legs and with one of her thread-like fingers she shows you her teeth.

You do not know what to say. So, you say, "They're beautiful."

She smiles at you largely. "Brand new," she says as she wiggles her arms back around, takes both her sticks, and stretches against the bench seatback. She seems relaxed. She almost leans against you, taps the pouch on your backpack—the place where you put the bolts—and says, "Elbowroom." Then she slides downward, limply bearing her shoulders over her sticks, as if a marionette on its rods.

It is a good time to withdraw; now you look out the window. It is good that you did, because here at last is your stop. Glenwood. You stand, quickly catching your backpack over your shoulder you walk to the front of the bus. The old woman grasps at a backpack strap and pulls on it. She nods and you try to say good-bye
 but you do not say it, and she lets go of the strap. She points a stick toward Bob Brindle's Bundles of Bargain Barn, shaking it, says, "Good buys." You turn, go to the door. It opens, you step down from the bus. You're glad to be done with all of everything on it.

Over there is a shabby aluminum shelter. You stand inside it mute. Outside, the sun is hot. The walls are glass; cracked from kick and boot. A broken florescent lamp dangles like a heat burst thermometer. The ceiling is rusty. There's a bench—three legs; one a stack of bricks. You chose not to sit. There is a dampness; a pungent wetness. The rain of days ago is unevaporated. Broad plants ramble between the narrow crevices like palmate creatures. You are the last dying fish in a draining aquarium.

About Your Kaleidoscope

So over there, faraway diagonally across the unapproachable parking lot is Bob Brindle's Barn of Bargains. The distance to it is flat and deserted: a black asphalt ocean; a dark desert stilled by abandonment. You head there, across the lot. On the way the air is hot; maybe hotter than that of the city. Your empty backpack feels heavy as if a dufflebag full of steal weighed on your shoulders. Would it be that the strange gifts from the old woman were swelling into wrought iron ingots? You refuse that absurd notion. Instead, a hidden place in the cool shade under the bushes beneath the tree behind the building back where you came from, where Richie stands, comes to mind. That imagining makes it possible to get across the parking lot.

Here now are the doors. They open with a sucking whoosh. Chilling, refreshed air swirls and passes around you. Mrs. Schpeidreck and the Puerto Rican man should have this air. You enter. The doors close. You stand. Someone walks around. You peer through cupped hands into the store. You are an astronomer, discovering new stars. Bright, rectangular, fluorescent lights are newer stars. If you had your kaleidoscope you would turn the lens and make it all into a three-cornered cosmos full of multicolored star clusters. But you will not think about your kaleidoscope now, because you have become an astronaut. At this instant you launch into a boundless, luminous universe. It is a gigantic, spacious place, but you do not feel unaccompanied. You are with a purpose; a simple want. You feel escorted. The generousness brings you to a delightful place. No, you cannot say openly why at this moment you have a cozy, snug feeling. You feel relaxed in this enormously private space.

There were clouds in the ceiling. No, they are not clouds, they are banners. Lovely drapes hang from the arches, ornamental wreaths of sale bargains. Radio angels broadcast sensuous announcements.

Now it is a cathedral. Holy music pours down upon you. Cool, soothing air baptizes you. You walk; more like drifting. Easeful, white lights escort you reverently into the silver center. You go deeper into the canyon of pews.

They are not pews; they are long, shelf-lined corridors—high stacked kiosks. You do not disagree that these tall aisles are the deep furrows, the soaring tops, the green-tasseled garlands of the grassy fields when you were young. You can pass between them easily. You flow effortlessly through the shelving maze comfortable that it is not complex; you may have been here before.

A young salesman appears. You do not say he is not magical. He is dressed in a cassock. He smiles kindly. He reaches forward asking, "Can I bless you?" Yes, he is attractive with his symmetrical hair, shapely eyes, and charming lips. And, the curiousness is not easily dismissed, his teeth are like those of the old woman on the bus, superbly flawless. Though, like the old woman, he is difficult to hear. He asks you again, "Can I bless you?" You think he thinks he thinks have not understood.

You do not say you have not, so you say, *yes*. You show him the coupon booklet and say that you are here to receive your free toaster. He takes the booklet helpfully from you like an usher at a theater. He opens it to the pages listing the appliances. He removes the coupon from the booklet with a nonchalant tearing.

You distress. You say *you removed the coupon from the booklet! It will be voided!*

"That's fine," he says, "removal will not void you." He returns the booklet, less one coupon. "I'll guide you." You follow him to the kitchen appliance area, and when there, he promptly displays a row of toasters.

"Presto! Joy!" Using your coupon like a joss stick, he wafts it over the toasters, that maybe it spreads incense. He taps on the shelf. "Blessed are these unique choices."

You wish that the humming radio angels above did not hum so loudly. You begin to feel less comfortable in this less now than heavenly place, this colossal store of Bob Brindle's. You want to lie down on your back between the aisles like the rows of grass so long ago and let the wind swish be silent. It is difficult hearing the salesman.

He stands aside, his arms apart, "These will sanctify your happiness?"

There's disappointment on that shelf, not happiness. Here are three tedious, pea-green, fatigued boxes, dull as milk. The grinning salesman waits handsomely. Trying to use words in a way that he uses, you say, *I had come to believe that this hollowed temple would present something more exotic, more ornate*. Your backpack seems to become heavier, as if filling with sand. You cast away the thought of bolts. You do not want your dissatisfaction to be visible, so you ask, *Is it just this. These?*

"These are the only appliances included with your coupon offer. The only free ones." The clerk seems amused, like he's smirking. You say to him, *they are identical and dull*. The clerk's smirk turns tart, "Free appliances don't come with many accessories," he sours. "I can, however, show you an upgrade. You'll get a twenty-percent discount."

Cringing, you polite him with, *oh, no, thank you*. You do not want to appear inconsiderate, so you play your fingers into one of the deep toasting slots, as if trying to make friends with someone's cat that doesn't show that it likes

About Your Kaleidoscope

you. You decide upon, *I suppose I'll have to take one of these. Right?*

"Yes. When you do, I'll be ready to help you check out." He vanishes in the same way he appeared, pleasing and loyal.

You stand alone now, helplessly, choosing among the ordinary. No radio angels beyond sing comfort. No cloud banners above float favor. What was once an astonishing cathedral has become banal. No toaster here beckons want. Tiny beads of displeasure form on your forehead. You do not fade from crying. You look downward, tears of defeat drop. You wish for change. Oh, to behold something new.

What is that? You're lifting your head; you're wiping your eyes. Something has changed, there are many, many pink flashing lights winking way down there at the distant end of the aisle. Faraway down the narrow aisle, deep inside a purple shadow a blinking light flickers, as if a sparkle within a long cavern. You do not ignore that the twinkling is for you.

It's a dazzling beckoning. You walk toward the aisle's end, and at last, enter into that cavern. It is a cavern filled with all shapes and sizes of televisions. Rows and columns of monitors are linked together, each displaying the same picture. Columns of television silhouettes ascend from floor to ceiling as if climbing a chain. They fill the large wall, multiplying. Each screen contains within it a likeness to another. The images curve, rotate and squirm in unison, soundlessly. Their whirling is the curl of bee larva inside a honeycomb.

Those television pictures are not bees at all. They are astronauts. They roll capriciously in outer space, inside the television. Each wears a silvery-frosted space suit.

You have never seen so many astronauts. The televisions expand in unison until the screen fills with the same smiling astronaut. One astronaut winks at you. One flirting. Another swelling largely as if when reaching the screen's edges he might climb out. You are captured. The astronauts seduce you with their ethereal smiles, as if they had brought those smiles with them all the way from some special, lovely planet. Smiles, like free coupons, that could be exchanged for cosmic pleasure unreservedly. Everywhere throughout the entire television salesroom there are more astronauts inside more televisions, each spaceman in a tube capsule, tied to an umbilical cord. The decorative arm emblems on their spacesuits, the shiny medals, were all given to them for their heroic explorations. They wave at you proudly because they know that you have affection for that accomplishment. You want to be in that space with those wonderful astronauts, floating around in that vaporous place inside the television. You understand them. Their

About Your Kaleidoscope

rolling in deep spaces is like you running through deep grasses. You yearn to be like them, dogpaddling in weightlessness, drifting in infinite happiness.

Then again, they seem troubled. Each astronaut is entombed in a vacuum, tethered to the television porthole by their spacesuit cables like balls to a paddle. This appreciation makes you sad. Just as when the rubber band on the ball-and-paddle game from your mother snapped, and the paddle with the wide-mouthed hippopotamus became lost. What did you do? What can you do? Can they find their way out, those teeming astronauts? Not by swimming, or maybe running or perhaps by cutting the space cord, then float free from inside the television screen? You are not unafraid to take one of them home, release an astronaut from its confine.

A clerk nears; one not unlike the one with the toasters. You say you are worried about the astronauts; *that* astronaut, pointing at it. You ask whether you can take it home and comfort it. And, that maybe it might also comfort you that perhaps you too could float around in. You and an astronaut?

The clerk agrees. "If you had that TV, you would receive joy and pleasure watching it." He taps the television, your television, as if it was you. With his elbows propped on the top, he rests his chin into his hands. "Bliss can easily be accomplished with one of these." You do not want to know if he winked at you. "Certainly, you will agree with that?"

You do not disagree. He cradles the television and carries it sympathetically to the counter. You do not know whether to follow, but you do. But nearer to the counter, you hesitate. Why now do you feel as if you have to say that you already have two televisions at home in your closet, the monitors gray and shady. Your broken toaster sits between them. You wonder if the clerk should know they do not play, and when they did, the picture was all just hazy pictures and interweaving jumbles that zigzagged dizzily. It would not have been unlike looking through your kaleidoscope. When those televisions did function, they played malicious sex, terrible comedy, and vague news. It was good when they stopped doing that. You do not think about your kaleidoscope while going where the clerk is.

The clerk waits. When get to the counter, his face brightens. He says, "Here's an idea." He says you won't have to pay right now. That later will be fine. "Credit. Same as cash" He's rubbing the screen, cleaning the screen. "Ninety days."

Ninety days will be long time to have to pay. You wonder if the astronauts will wait inside the television for three months. You ask, *will everything be the same?*

About Your Kaleidoscope

"No." The clerk explains. "You won't have to pay until ninety days."

The idea that you must take ninety days to pay is an unfeasibly lengthy time. It could be cold and rainy weather then, maybe ice. Cloudy. It might be weather that Richie cannot be outside. Three months. You do not know about three months.

You say, *I do not want to come back out here again on the bus, not in three months.* The clerk does not realize about how it was with the old woman and her sticks, the turban man and the butterflies, the puzzling lady in the sun glasses. They were not pleasing.

"You can take it with you now. You can pay later."

Everything here goes nervously. Looking behind, the astronauts hover. They hang, they float. They suspended silvery, swaying tenderly from their spaceman threads like precious ornaments. Now they do not seem move about as they were. They, too, seem anxious. You worry more. You do not wish for them to remain in that shadowy suspense like that, certainly not in that suspenseful way, hovering that way, suspended unwanted. You wonder if this clerk is sympathetic.

But there the television sits. The clerk rests on it patiently, uncomplaining that the astronauts inside it are not.

You do not want to think about your ride out to Glenwood. So much Glenwood today. But now is the time to do something. This deciding moment is like when to open the mailbox, like determining where Mrs. Schpeidreck is, like resolving past the Puerto Rican man. Deciding is whether to speak to Richie. Isn't not to decide a decision?

So you do decide. You take the coupon booklet out of your backpack and hand it to the clerk. You say you want to buy it now because you're afraid that something might happen in the meantime. The astronauts might drift away to another place.

The salesman says it'll all be okay. "They'll still be there."

You do not wish to be undoubtful, so you announce *I want it now.*

For a moment the clerk eyes you with what you sense is an understanding watch. Can he see that you made a passionate choice? He helps you, "Don't forget the thirty-three percent discount. A Bob Brindle discount! Go ahead," he seems to cheer, "you can have it now." You reach for the television.

"Oh, no." The clerk takes it away. That's right. There you go." The newer check seems brighter than the first, the yellow sunny and cheerful. The numbered words, delighted.

"Okay," says the clerk. He snaps the check into the cash drawer. It closes its mouth around it.

You leave Bob Brindle's Bundle of Bargain Barn with your happy cardboard treasure chest. The television is squeaking comfy inside its Styrofoam cradle.

Things are going well. The Glenwood #67 arrives after just a few minutes sitting in that broken-down bus shelter. You get in and pick out the same seat, halfway to the back of the bus, behind the handicapped railing, under the package rack, and away from the driver. Two college kids come on and sit too near you. Your backpack is over your shoulders and you hold your TV prize tightly on your lap. The students talk about earrings and sex. After a while, they get off. A too fat girl in a sleeveless blouse lumbers on and sits right behind driver. Her breasts are like Aunty Marty's, but the girl is just a teenager. She turns in her seat and stares straight at you until, finally, when your street comes up and you rise to get off, she touches you at the door and asks, "Do you have astronauts in that box?"

"*No,*" you lashed too abruptly. "*It's none of your business anyway.*" You jump to the sidewalk, hurrying to your apartment you wonder if Richie will be outside. You cannot imagine how Richie would not be inside his fence.

But, you will be content if he is, but you will less content if he notices you.

Richie is there. He stands facing westward. The sun will set too soon. Does he hear you? Yes he does and he turns around, but he does not look. He asks, "Is it three o'clock? Is it three o'clock?" As you come near, squinty eyes act as if watching. His eyelids flicker blindly, blinking faster as you walk, like something behind them was chewing at his eyelids. He can hear. He can shout. He can pluck the fence posts. He can follow the sun. He can wiggle out of a black plastic bag naked. He can wear Mrs. Schpeidreck's dead husband's clothes. He can tremble when his father scolds so cruelly. He can ask the time. He can worry about rain. But he cannot see.

Approaching him you say, *Yes, Richie, it's almost three o'clock*. You do not feel guilt that you have told him a lie, but you regret that he is unable to see your new television. He plucks the fence points rapidly when you get near your apartment door. Can he hear your astronauts? It is unhopeful that Mrs. Schpeidreck and the Puerto Rican notice you. Success. You go upstairs; into your apartment. Close the door shut safely.

This is an exciting moment, this brand-new television. Plug it in. Be careful not to use the bad outlet. Adjust the little antennas; the ones like insect feelers. The screen

About Your Kaleidoscope

flashes. There's nothing but grey space. This saddens you. You thought the picture would not look like your old one—fuzzy and grey. Now abruptly, silvery-pink explosions foam across the screen followed by rising black lines, then clarity. A sexy woman dances in loose clothing; her mouth opens and closes voluptuously. She sings a song about savage ambivalence that you think you understand. Her elbows rise happily, showing you that deodorant erases sadness.

Where are the astronauts? Did they float away on the bus? Where is your astronaut? The one that had winked at you; the one out of so many seduced only you. You change the channel. A glossy mouth with spotless teeth says that buying large pieces of gum will remove misery. Perhaps your disappointment can be eliminated with chewing-gum. The big, bright teeth say yes. It is synthetic. You have seen it on the bus. Switch to another channel. Search through the ethereal screen for your astronaut helpers. You continue to search, but they cannot be seen. Changing to a channel helplessly, there someone tries to give away simple contentedness but they soon too are swallowed inside vapor and buzzes. Another channel? A handsome torso appears telling you about ugly news. For a moment his image is clear, the he transforms into an elliptical contour, as if seen through your kaleidoscope. Horizontal ribbons undulate and the handsome torso fall into the hollow television bottom. Then appear ugly news stories as told by a handsome torso. His image is clear for a moment, then his torso transforms into eclipsing stripes. Waves of horizontal ribbons undulate up from the screen, and he falls into what you think is the hollow television bottom. It is the frolicsome astronauts you want; the ones you bought, and yearn for.

You do not avoid your anger. For some untimed moments you tramp in irritable circles around your apartment. Without thought of consequence, you step in front of the television and violently slap it. Slap it. Slap it. Now harder. You do not care about stopping, but you do. You are satisfied that your hand does not hurt.

The television screen shutters, blinks stunned, like something bewildered, like Richie when the sun goes behind a cloud. A vaporous haze dims. A grayness suspends. A shadow not unlike a night without moon or stars, darkens.

There is a blank image, mesmerizing in its emptiness. Then, ever so slowly, as if awakening from a trance, a specter slowly appears. Fleeting astral images ripple; a blurred rainbow undulates. They become waves; waves lapping at the screen's periphery like those breaking on a shore, summoning you from the beach to come into the

About Your Kaleidoscope

water. A voice from the television speaks, "You cannot swim, but if you swim in here, you will be carried away unthreatened."

The mesmery enchants you, just as the tall grasses in the wheaty fields behind your house enchanted. You go into that little television and soon you are paddling in space just the way the astronauts did. You swim among the waves, the rows, drifting happily. You do not care now that you are alone. With the switch of a channel you can become a beetle, a pigeon, a cloud, pleased to be any one of them. You do not care if your mother, or Aunt Marty, could see you here inside this happy screen. You do not care that now you are outward and visible. It is you there, inside that television. You are without astronauts, without your Aunt Marty up there on the porch, without your mother asking so inquisitively about how you are being now. Here, inside this television, you can run through the tall grasses, grasses full of whisper, grasses full of forget. You do not think about your kaleidoscope.

The television screen glazes over, casting a haze across the screen in the same manner that clouds close together when they know a storm will follow. A tenuous wind blows. The tall grasses wave as if some unseen thing is running through them.

Into The Flame

It was how the match was struck, its imposing approach to the wick. It was the gradual flickering to brightness that made the lone candle, the modest celebratory cake, and the charmingly decorated gift beside it reflect a worried glimmer from Brian's eyeglasses. As seen up close, the manner in which Brian pinched the flaming match between finger and thumb, as if a miniature wand, the way he seemed to hold it overly expressive, made Clarette see his face much too scarlet. From across the table, from Clarette's watching, Brian's lighting motions kindled a distant memory, warningly, and set a sorrowful remembrance ablaze.

Although a generation and a half had elapsed since that memory, it had an invisible linger, ready at any time to light, like the subdued pilot flame in the kitchen stove behind her. As she watched Brian rouse the candle's flame, it also roused much more. The recollection that far-away winter night came to her in the way the candle wick came to blaze; without hurry. And in a manner, uninvited.

Just as Brian had come to her—without hurry. And,

some extent, invited. He offered vigilant patience, an easygoing devotion, and unreserved intimacy, astonishing her that she could love again. On the night of gift and cake and candle lighting, they were celebrating her fiftieth birthday; their third anniversary. An anniversary tentatively explained inside the tiny kitchen of her house, and outside to others elsewhere, as "seeing each other."

The light flickered gradually, the glimmer brightened. Clarette could have know the memory it revealed was there, but it came unexpected, and she wished it would not come now, as if it was an uninvited guest who'd come to her birthday celebration from the vaporous past and inappropriately presented her with a long-lost photograph whose image brought grief. Because in that imaginary picture is her Poppa—*forever and always her Poppa*—with his generous palms holding steady around her small hands, pressing them together with increasing tightness as he stares over the frozen lake, watching helplessly as the unhindered fires burn sinisterly.

Confusing Clarette's vacant gaze as reticence about his gift, Brian pushed it forward timidly. He grinned in that preposterous, gracious beam that had been the first thing that had collapsed her barriers.

But Clarette did not see his shine; her eyes were pinned in a hypnotic fix that remained within the glow at the candle's center. To divert her, Brian imitated blowing. The candlelight appeared teased by Brian's mimicked puffs. It flickered obstinately. As if encouraged by the taunt, the glowing aura inside the flame wavered more bright. From it, images of the past swelled further: silhouetted cloud shadows; cyclone smoke plumes; a high yellow flame, its long jaundiced reflection begging contemptuously over the ice, summoning her Poppa.

Brian picked up the candle, held it for Clarette, said time was up, that he'd make a wish for her. He blew out the flame. The smolder wisped upward between them, indifferently. Clarette's distant expression disquieted him. His grin dropped. He put the candle down.

Clarette stared into the fainting ember. It dimmed, and the memory-aura retreated the way it had arrived, uninvited. As it disappeared, it left behind the sound her Poppa made as he tried to use the only language the malady of age had left him capable of speaking—he wept.

During the early years of her half of the generation, when Clarette was young in it, the future seemed as inaccessible as a stubborn lidded box. Then, yet so young, and even at times now, she doesn't think it's such a childish simile. Because, eventually, and often at unexpected times, that box was opened, its secretive contents revealed, and the impatient past no longer prudently undisclosed. Even into adolescence, as maturity nudged her clumsily forward, she held to the box simile. Still does, at fifty.

Throughout, each successive opening continues to return childhood memories. It might be a place, a thing—some people—that would transport her. Sometimes it would be to her grandfather's house; more often, Christmas mornings. All those garnished packages and trimmed boxes down there under the tree. She'd be upstairs on her bed eagerly alert while her parents slept blithely. The impatient wait until all would be prudently undisclosed, accepted.

Well into adulthood, while in wait for something—a thing, a person, a place to be—she'd reminisce on the expectations of her youth. How they'd felt. The anticipation. Their findings. She took it as prophetic, analogous. They helped her receive humbly the conclusion when it came.

Places: that etched event—her first piano recital. Seated tiny at an enormous piano, on a high and broad bench as if perched on the dining room table at home, she waited. The forever it took for the curtain to rise; but in the end, the encouraging applause. Another forever: at highschool graduation where students received their diplomas alphabetically, the infinite delay until *VanVolkinburg* was called. Then, not much later, at the veterinarian's office—all that rolling and kicking had to be more than one. There were five.

Things: a small thing—the mailbox. The proofs were not in it, but were soon delivered full of astonishing praise. A large thing: that dilapidated farm house—the impatience over unhurried workmen; the rushed housewarming later. Memories spurred by things. Like the way Brian had held the match.

People: those at the wedding—so many adoring friends. The things *they* gave. Things that now do not spur. Special people: Clarette will not argue that her pregnancy was unquestionably the longest wait, and the one with the most exciting closure. Baby Katherine. More than adoring. Beyond astonishing.

Not all that came out of that stubborn-lidded box were joyful. Sorrowful futures had come forth and when they did, Clarette pitied Pandora, felt her panic as she tried to press down hard on a lid that would not close. In that way, in other ways, it was not an easy conclusion to accept with humility a future that did not go humbly back into the box. There was a marriage unveiled—how contentedly she'd encouraged him to pursue his own quite path, until she found out jealously where it had taken him. Those years she spent cultivating her practice, seeing her clients grow, waiting for it to flourish—the lawsuit that poisoned it. And then, not so far in her past that the recollection has dulled, she'd learned that a bold present can disguise a meek past, unveiling an undeniable future just as crippling as that which the disease paralyzes—Huntingdon's.

To-date, and throughout Clarette's past, the impatient uncertainties of her future, however, were largely kind. To her comfort, when uncovered, the present revealed a smaller, less doubtful future, and ensured for her an enduring past; at least a past with willful memories. She held this thought: as long as nothing turned up between futures, the present wouldn't be cursed with what hadn't happened. In her childhood, so full of future then, Clarette did not know there were pasts that had happened, unknowns waiting until the future, which were yet to be revealed.

Now, when Clarette opens a new door, she leaves the one behind ajar. Because when the future arrived with unexpected revelations and puzzling disclosures, as they did when she was young, she trusts sincerely that the present will progress with encouragement. And, if not, at least its progress could be full of wish.

"Hey!" Brian broke Clarette's stare. "You didn't make a wish." He licked his fingertips, pinched the candle wick. "But you still got cake," and gave it a sympathetic push forward. Pensively, she watched it come to her and wondered if her future with Brian was in progress. She'd come on board with him well into mid-journey.

When Clarette was a nine-year-old, she and her Poppa took a train across Pennsylvania. Between Pittsburgh and Altoona was the Horse-Shoe Curve. They sat by the window in a car at the center of the train. When it was at the sharpest of the curve, from the middle of the train, Clarette could see both the engine and the last car as they rounded the tight bend. Where was she sitting with Brian?

Clarette halved the cake, offered forks. As they finished, Brian politely slid Clarette's gift across the table. She gazed at the prettily decorated box, studied its enchanting smallness. Took in apprehensively its veiled largeness. The contents of this gift might disclose an uncertain future.

With uneasy fingers she struggled clumsily to unfasten the trimming Brian had tied into an awkward bow until the knot began to loosen. Brain reached over to help, pulling at wrapping and ribbons until the lid opened just fine.

There inside the box, nested in soft tissues, was a hugely rounded ring, gilded, as if a gold-plated steel washer. Through it, a threaded bolt protruded. Attached to that was an extravagant adornment: a gold falcon spread fan-like wings outward, its head turned upward, its mouth aggressively agape, its eyes focused acutely on something faraway—as if to chase it and catch it in its beak.

Clarette exploded with joy. Breathlessly, impatiently, yet elegantly, she drew it out as if she was examining a luxurious antique pocketwatch presented to her by a jeweler; but it was not at all a watch. A brassily extravagant hood ornament now lay in her palm. It was an engine hood trophy; one that at one time had been proudly mounted atop the enormous chrome radiator of a 1929 Persch-LaFrance pumper fire truck.

She cupped it with both hands, as if it were indeed that jeweler's watch. But much, much more. She brought the ornament to her lips, kissed it, and looked at Brian, "Oh, Brian!" Then, forgetting momentarily that he was there, she kissed Brian.

He leaned back in his chair, put his hands behind his head, beamed with his magnificent grin, and leaned back in his chair, as if to get a larger view of her enthusiasm.

She cradled his gift to her chest. "Do you know what this means?"

Of course he did. "You've been looking for that one for a long time," confirming to her his devoted attentiveness.

She examined it for a second time, as if unconvinced that it really was what it was, and when no more suspicion could deny her pleasure, she rose out of her chair, nearly levitated, surged across the table at Brian; the celebratory cake all but squashed; the frosting leaving an alluring daub. Stretching all the way to him, she kissed again, and hugged his neck, his head. She leaned fully into him. She held the precious 1929 ornament tucked tight between her breasts, its beak inside Brian's ear.

Brian now abundantly embraced, Clarette shrank back into her chair. She put the gold falcon up to her cheek, as if like a found baby bird, she would feel its heart beating. There, holding it face-to-face, with the falcon's head gleaming brightly, its wings spreading further, its golden eyes glistening fiercely, she wept.

Bufflehead

Until this day, Danny Furman had been upside right. But because things hadn't gone well at all, it was now Danny Furman who was now upside down, buried with heartache and pain.

His belly, usually downward with a soft-middle slouch, was in a tight lodge between the steering wheel and the seat, and now that belly slumped upward. Tucked between all of those—seat, tummy, wheel—and squeezed like a rubbery gasket was the floor mat.

An elbow pressed the brake pedal; a leg hung above the headrest. His other leg, the one he could still move, was propped expectantly against the door-lever, forcing it ajar so it wouldn't swing closed and squish his ankle as it had done the last time he'd given the door a fierce kick to keep it open. His eyes, ears, and face—*his whole head, for chrissake*—were gorged with the load of wrong-way-down blood, filling as if water balloons about to burst. His trapped knee twitched like a pinched grasshopper. His left arm, cocked halfway as if a partly opened jackknife, was just as useless in that angled position. The curved shift rod would have soon become a steel noose if he hadn't slackened its neck-throbbing clench by intermittently wagging his head loose. His face was much too near to where the heater's spiky fan blades might sever the pimples on his forehead like lawn-blades at weed roots; or, if he moved any closer, cut his cheek and slice apart his many freckles like a serrated dot-to-dot. At any other time, his curly red hair spiraled outward, but then, on that day of jaggy metal and achy necks, his curls dangled downward, as if an unwrung mop. Twisted like he was, Danny Furman felt like that; like something ready for the wringer.

    He could, however, use his right arm. Which he did, cautiously moving the hand at the end of it. He pulled it up, licked the pair of slices where he'd cut two fingers trying to reach around, between, behind, under the shaver-sharp metal track of the ashtray.

    Indeed, an ashtray. His car was from an age where drivers could smoke comfortably. It was one of those later-models with crank-up windows, knobs that turn, even a cigarette lighter that when it was pushed in, glowed into a quick sizzling blaze until it shorted out the dash lights. Then the radio. Danny doesn't smoke, but because he needs dash lights and a radio, he'd stuffed chewing gum into the fuse-clip. A compact car even for those days, made yet more compact by his misshaped constriction. *Damn*, it was painful.

But, *gosh*, it was a great view. Danny could see everything clearly: the ganglion of colored wires; the black-tape-wrapped connectors; the twisted cables; and those stupid fucking pinchy things that when he pushed them together never came apart unless he squeezed them really hard between his teeth.

Checking his finger injuries, he probed his only moveable hand back into and among the dashboard jumble, trying again to grapple a pair of cables loose. Eyes closed, using his fingers like pliers, he jimmied the wires unsighted until they freed just a single wire, which in that manner handily offered access to all the other ganglions of unidentified wires.

Wiring blindly. That's exactly how Danny had to do it because just after he'd started the wiring, he remembered that he hadn't brought real pliers under there and even if he had he probably would have dropped them too far under the seat and couldn't have reached them anyway unless he unscrewed himself from that dashboard hole, found the pliers jammed in the seat crack, and re-threaded himself back under the dashboard to get back at the wires. He couldn't do that. Not now. No way. Not enough time. He has to do what he has to do *now*. Obstinately, with the only tools available: his fingers—now, two bloodied fingers.

And do it quickly. By afternoon he needed to fix the radio, connect it to the antenna (the decade-aged car had no CD player, just a bootlegged satellite receiver) and tie all the snarled wiring back into its original knot, unfasten himself from his twisted position, pick his tools off the driveway, write Randall a begrudged check for half the rent, pack the car, and then drive away; out to where Mallorie was.

Do it furtively. Attentive. He had to keep an ear for the mail truck, a leg out for Mr. Oliver Pennick, and an eye out for his help. Although any help that Mr. Oliver Pennick would suggest would be offered splendidly, Danny at least knew that. But he didn't need Mr. Oliver Pennick's assistance then, any of Mr. Oliver Pennick now.

While he wiggled wires for their unsuccessful connection, Danny knew fully that he should've done all of this sooner, and not how he was.

The packing that is, not the wiring. But Danny couldn't get started then. He'd had other things to do. Like, gather stuff. Packing it together in his unsystematic manner; heaping it together out there on the driveway like a bird collecting bits for nesting. Of course, when he was done, he'd unpack it. Then he'd re-pack it again just to make sure that indeed he had—packed it away in Danny Furman fashion.

But, it was late in the morning by the time Danny carried the majority of his things out, down to the driveway, and then set them haphazardly around the perimeter that he began working on the radio. He'd tried hard to do what was needed to be done in a time shorter than the sum of their lengths, and do it so that he could leave unhurried. To compound urgency, all the tasks had to be completed before the mail truck arrived. Around noon. Here, the way it was, at eleven-thirty, things looked as if he wasn't going to get any of them done. It wasn't that he had a great deal to pack—most of it the unwanted stuff of yardsales that even the spendthrift would pass—but nevertheless, invaluable his stuff.

Scattered across the driveway like unclaimed airport luggage was: a cardboard file box, two lamps with incompatible hand-made shades, a pitiful suitcase, four liquor-store boxes crammed with jumble, those aging comic books that at no age will attract collector , a cracked coffee maker, and a tattered atlas—yellow marker-lined by someone unknown. Plenty of rubberband bound papers, some half-burned candles, the dish rack—with pots, platters, pans, plates clacking un-stored in their Rubbermaid cages. An upholstered rocking chair—its worth assessed only in the currency of nostalgia.

Yet, there's more. Some still up there in his apartment: the milk crate full of wood blocks; and a wastebasket full of it.

Neither unclaimed nor mislaid is his chest of whittle and carving chisels. And chief among all his possessions, as if a trophy cup to an athlete, his dufflebag of treasures.

But, first-things-first. This was Danny's self-asserted morning order: get the radio working. Although later, following his declaration, he felt bewildered by the heaps of ordered *firsts* left around firstly and began again, secondly.

Here he was, twisted under the dashboard, legs a droop out the car door. A tousled mound of belongings lay heaped for the trunk; the hood wide-agape like a pelican's nib, ready to swallow all into it.

If an unaware person should come upon the scene, it might appear as if there'd been a wreck, an automobile accident, a car rolled, things spilled. A body, trapped inside. *'Hurry, somebody call 911.'*

Danny couldn't call 911. Not from his cell phone. It's stubbed between the car seat: battery dead, charger lost, server expired, neglected—a phone as useful as a stone in a poker ante.

To Danny, packing-up, fixing, was the way things simply get done, but never just *simply*. Pull on a wire and see what happens. Guess work; discover the solution by blunder the way someone fumbles in the dark without a flashlight. Everything all over the place, scattered, or, everything put into a box, mixed—always more Danny Furman out than Danny Furman in.

Like his red hair. It does not hang, it coils. Great whorls spiral loosely from behind his ears. Curls leap off the top of his head, then ring around his shirt collar as if a bundle of rusty springs had slacked from their fasteners. He is not tall, but his high looped hair makes him seem vertical. He is twenty-seven years old, but those pink freckles dotting his wide face will make you think that he was still in the fifth grade. When he speaks, an extensive mouth and dense lips will outline his words broadly. He'll pause between words, and giving you a sideward glance, his wide-apart eyes will blink slow and darkly, in the manner of an owl. He won't notice when someone looks at his bowed nose that slide-curves outward like a mallard's bill between his puffy cheeks, but he'll get defensive if there's a remark made about his forehead; the premature furrow along the center. Randall says he looks like a duck. Or, as he had said spitefully when Danny said he was moving out, "like a fucking clown".

Danny's slender muscle-less arms, his soft shoulders, and his supple tummy might convey an impression of weakness, being unhealthy. He is not. On the contrary, because of his erratic and flighty lifestyle, full of symbiotic survival and avian-like existence, he is that bird—a duck, a lark. He's durable, so when the decisive end arrives, he'll endure, crawling from the apocalypse healthy, breaking free from inside a new shell.

Before he'd wriggled there under the dashboard, he'd known the going wasn't going to be easy. He considered the sensibility of what he had to do. Its logic. After which, he'd decided to make the wiring job the last thing to do. Later often gave a better sense of timing. He'd load the trunk, pack the back seat, then fix the antenna; yes, that's what he'd do.

He surveyed his belongings, assessed their geometry, forecasted a priority. He couldn't load the toolbox; it had the tools he needed for wiring. He couldn't pack the coffeemaker or the atlas now. Although he certainly knew how to get to Mallorie's new apartment, the atlas was his paperback GPS. The coffeemaker? It had to go in so that it could go out first. He decided on the lamps. The ones whose shades he'd made out of varnished newsprint, then laminated with bird tracings. Of course they would need some extra care packing, some special padding so things wouldn't get crushed.

For that he had just the right padding: Easter grass. It was up the stairs into the apartment, back in the bedroom, inside the closet, stowed furtively in the back corner. The tune *three bags full* came into his head as he climbed the stairs. He opened the closet door and there they were— three large, disturbingly ebony, bags. Each indeed full. Bright virescent shredded ribbons; the jade-green plastic slivers in which chocolate rabbits, pink marshmallows, pastel jellybeans, dyed eggs could be nested. Although in lieu of holiday baskets, the Easter grass was stuffed inside coroner's bags. It was a sinister trick that Randall had filled the bags with newsprint and treated Halloweeners with. Where he'd gotten them, Danny never asked. It was just something *that Randall* got. The paper emptied, Danny packed them with the remnants of workplace discards: shiny green flakes; slippery polyethylene grass clippings. The coroner bag's zipper did not zip fully; some of the Easter grass bunched among the linking, stressing the seam with a mysterious stretch. Cinched within a tie wire was a tuft of frayed strands that protruded goofily, a fake-grass headdress on an immense head. An orange cord bound them from bursting. They were more the farcical trick of Halloween than the basket treat of Easter.

"I get it at work," Danny would tell those who'd asked

it. Then, after he answered, he'd close his eyes, roll his head like a crow looking about, and wait for the predictable *how come* question. To which he'd answer sardonically, as if to him, the question from the asker was rhetorical, that the answer was something everyone but the asker did not comprehend, "Because it's there and I can."

Then, always, that third question: *Where?*

Gesturing in whatever direction he supposed it was in relationship to where he stood with the asker the time, he'd offer the answer with dramatic obviousness, presupposing that the place was a well-known landmark: "Loringer Plastics." It was, however, a landmark known only to Danny. When he described its location, most remarked with surprise; they didn't know there was actually any sort of activity across the bush-tangled creek, up that driveway-scrapings of a road, in that squat concrete building the color of used bandage at the far end of town.

"Yep." Then adding to his short answer indifferently, and to prove that they didn't know that something went on there, "Three shifts."

Danny is a Loringer rotational lineman, the one who adjusts any one of the machines that cut and press and slice and roll the chloroprene, or vinylidene, or methacrylate pellets—or, whatever *plastic-ene* word Danny feels like using during the *where* or *how come* questions—that arrive in room-sized crates and are dumped, spilling like marbles from a box, into the grinding hopper at loading dock of that squat concrete building at the end of the road-chipping road that manufactures artificial grass for Easter baskets. Or, that soft packing for grocery tomatoes. Sometimes, depending upon orders, he'll set the machine to stamp out those little green strawberry containers, vegetable packs, perforated grape sacks, and whatever else the current client has requested, just as long as they're happy that it's in translucent green.

Discarded outputs, bad castings, second, he takes home. The vegetable bags for trash, the tomato boxes for his woodcarving tools, and the Easter grass for packing. Yes, they're frivolous perks, he knows that, but nobody else he knows gets perks like those. It's a wily job. He considers a career in employment satirically, and stubbornly proud of the ploy. He enjoys the puzzlement it gives his friends, the ones with youthful-dutiful jobs; the ones with focused career goals, with resume-sensible occupations, with perks that aren't plastic leftovers. He explains it to them with a priggish tone, "I could be doing some other menial work, but not everyone can make Easter grass." He'd wink, but it'd give things away. "It's a special job."

In Danny's lexicon special meant, *a quirky day job*. Which includes a sub-definition, rarely vocalized but always under-toned, *"Believe it or not, I have greater desires, better plans, than making fucking tomato boxes, my friends."* They accept his rationale about the quirky day job, albeit with placated support. Danny comes back at them with, "Hey? Doesn't your job also just render down to simply getting a paycheck?" His work ambitions are not so linear, or tangible, or with any kind of duration. But always eclectic. Easily replaced. Never complex. In that context, he occasionally hands out the trick justification when the tone of the *how come* question carries a dubious intonation. *You do?* "Yep," following it with a brusque chop, "and I don't think a thorough explanation of what I have and do is necessary." Or did. Or keeps around.

Like his furniture. The ones sprayed out there on his driveway. There's a small worktable with two sun-frayed wooden lawn chairs he and Mallorie ("artfully" as he described it to Mr. Oliver Pennick) patched bottoms and armrests onto from her special assorted fabrics. The cloth seats are tucked politely under the worktable as if expecting dinners. Next to the chairs, a stained pillow sack stuffed with laundry, next to it, a swollen backpack crammed with still not yet worn used clothing. "Some things just don't need explanation," he'd say when asked about them. His things.

There are many things for which Danny plainly refuses to explain; the chronology of their acquisition, less plainly. His lawn chairs: a pair of sun-frayed wooden frames; how Mallorie recycled them with cushioned upholstery; the mixed-color fabrics. His toolbox: crammed inequitably with gear he'd scurried together from one place or another like a seabird pecking at the wash behind a retreating wave. The wicker rocker:.....The coroner bags: three of them, filled.

Of course, chiefly above all is Mallorie's sculpture. At first take, the sculpture suggests the coarseness of burlap, but when touched, the feel is of satin. Its shape is the contour is of a cursive written W. A pair of wing-like boughs resembles the vanes of a fan. They open broadly, bringing to mind fronds reaching upward—in manner of a Jack-in-the-Pulpit—with its reddened purple-veined cloth, ruffled pinions, feathered limbs, that curl upward and outward—or is it downward and into as Danny presumed at first? The folds begin their ascent from inside an urn (Danny marvels at her ceramic work, too) with a surreptitious unveiling; the widening hands akin to the enchanting way a magician opens the empty handkerchief, revealing the previously hidden thing inside it. Her sculpted magic captures adoration, rendering it kinetic. Mallorie said, "It keeps passion in a motionless time. It draws the viewer out of a small place, a tiny beginning, then into the open air, out to a greater place. A larger space."

But her description contrasts somewhat differently from what Danny initially had said he saw in the sculpture: although not entirely divergent. While lightly brushing the cloth, he said, "But, Mallorie, it looks like it's going in, coming together, gravitating. Going inward to the center of something. Those hands," he paused, turned to her, "is that what they are? Hands?" He'd asked it not so much for clarification, but a want to be sure, to have her appreciate his appreciation—that together they were like-minded artists.

"Wings," she suggested helpfully.

"Those wings," rubbing the tips, "I'll call them hands for now, are joining, coming together."

Are they hands or wings? The two images vary while Danny contemplates the distinction, either while lazing in bed staring at the sculpture, or while carrying it out to the car. If it is wings, of what sort of bird will take flight in his bedroom. If it is hands, they are Mallorie's, beckoning to him?

"They're going out," gesturing her hands into a shape of the meaning, making a prayer-like pose, and then fluttering them away, like the birds of sign-language. "But," she put her arm around his waist, "if you see it as coming together, that can be your experience of it, and that's okay too." Drawing him nearer, "That's what art is, Danny, the experience." Leaning harder into him, then after a second, bumping hard against him playfully, "But I'm sorry there, Buster; you're wrong." She put her hands on the frond tips, drew them away, and said, "I've called it, *Love Expands*." She pulled mischievously at the elastic around his pants. "Like this does. Expands. You need to eat more. You're as skinny as a stork."

Her artistic style is, as Danny described it summarily, "eclectic". He said her style has no genre. She was quick to correct him. "Oh, not at all. It's homogeneous....just art." She aimed a pair of scissors at the middle of his chest, acting dangerous, "There's no definition; the experience comes from the soul."

Before hands and fronds and purple-hued wings, there was no Mallorie. Danny met her inadvertently at Dot Your Eye, a coffeehouse-studio hangout for the caffeine-laced and pot-mellowed art students at Gilmore. The day is indubitable—doubly. It was a Tuesday; a day of both delight and contempt. Delight, because of Mallorie. Contempt, because it was the day he signed on as Randall's roommate.

In the beginning, Danny went there to be with artists. He figured if he wanted people to know he was one, he'd have to mix with them, show them he was viable, rub against them and see if any art got on him. Although the artist-students were a wee bit confused as to where Danny had come from, and what he had brought with him, they liked his palpable eagerness, and finally drawing him in, let him stand within their circle. Or sit, rather, around the sand pool.

The sand pool was just that: a pool filled with sand. Someone that nobody can remember who dragged an oversized plastic wading pool—the kind children splash in—into the Dot Your Eye. The same unknown someone had poured sand into it. At some point or other, everyone had had to sit around the sand pool talking about their work, kicking at the sand, barefooted, playing with plastic kiddie toys and mellowing out from the joint they'd just smoked outside by the pottery shack.

Danny felt initiated while sitting around it, sifting sand, talking about art stuff. He declined the pot smoking invitations. On his next visit around the sand pool Danny dumped a bag of his Easter grass into the center. The minced plastic strips annoyed some, but the stoner-artists got excited over it, mixing it with the sand, making it look like a seashore sand dune.

Mallorie was one of the annoyed ones.

A few days after Danny had put the Easter grass into the sand pool, he sat at the coffee bar talking with Roy. Roy was an older post-grad student who by being at the college for such a long time was the self-appointed supervisor, but was neither student nor supervisor. As they talked, Danny watched this girl step into the sand pool not barefooted but in sandals, and with a pasta colander sieved as many of the skinny green ribbons she could out of the sand, then packed them into a paper sack.

Danny interrupted Roy. "Who's the new girl over there by the sand pool?"

"That's Mallorie. Nice, uh?"

She came over to Roy with the paper sack, dropped it on a chair next to him. "Who put this plastic in the sand?"

Roy said, "I did."

Danny said, "No, I did."

She took up the sack again, gave them both a rueful glance. "Actually, I don't care who did. I just think it's annoying. There's enough plastic on a real beach without making it like that here."

Roy shrugged, looked behind him. "Like everything's actually real here?"

Mallorie rolled the sack into a bundle, tucked it under her arm like it was a lunch bag. "Where's the recycle box? This grass stuff might be recyclable."

Danny knew. "Outside by the pottery shack."

She looked at Danny, an expression that maybe she'd seen him before, grinned. "Great." She turned as if to go there, then turned back, held the bag for Roy to see. "Is that where you keep all the other grass?" She made a joint-to-mouth sign; her lips puckered too supple, making it obvious that they'd never actually puffed one.

"Yep."

She looked at Roy, then at the sack. "I don't think so. It's too clever for you." She tried Danny. "So, then this is your stuff?" She pulled her long hair around, held the back of her hand on her hip.

Danny was too enamored to confess fully so instead he said, "its stuff I get at work. They just throw it away anyway."

Handing it to Danny, "Here" She put it in his lap. "Maybe you can use it for something else." She turned and started to walk away, the long hair hiding hip pockets that swayed.

Danny faced Roy innocently, concealing something crafty. "What?" As if he'd had to ask.

Mallorie about-faced and came back and stood in front of Roy. "I can I have the table next week to set up my exhibits?"

"Sure," he said with self-officiousness. "You got it."

Danny circled on his seat, looked up at her and asked, "What's your exhibit?"

"Soft sculpture," she declared tidily. "Thanks for asking." She glared at Roy for not. "It's fabric form." She moved a pair of hands around an invisible figure-eight. "That's my genre. My device." Clearly eager to say something about it she continued, "It's cloth over wire, or sometimes wood, like tree branches and I like to..."

Roy interrupted by saying, "You can see some of her work at the colonnade." Danny thought Roy was going to say something praising about what he'd thought about what she did but he didn't.

"...like to decoupage...."

Roy ignored her and the word. "Mallorie has sorta taken over the studio out there like she'd moved in."

Mallorie dispensed Roy, now speaking to Danny, "...decoupage isn't actually what it is, more like fabric-Mache."

Roy held his palm out, as if introducing Mallorie on stage. He cuffed Danny on his shoulder and said, "Good work, but sorta like looking at laundry out to dry." Hand still on Danny, nodding at the paper sack, "Maybe you could make plastic-Mache out of that grass stuff?"

"Did you smoke any of it, Roy?" Mallorie did not make the joint-to-mouth sign again, although Danny wished she had. The fingers on her hands were like "Or were you just going to leave it there in the sand pool like some green shit in kitty litter."

"Green shit?"

"Yeah, green shit." Pointing at a shelf on the wall, "Like those lumps over there."

Roy did not turn to look, seemed like he knew where his work could be seen; didn't say anything more. Danny liked that a lot. Roy shut-off. Danny liked Mallorie a lot. The acerbic sarcasm; her feistiness toward Roy, the way she whittled him, making him smaller.

Mallorie took the bag away from Danny. "Here, maybe I'll keep this green shit anyway. Melt it down for something." A narrow tear at the bottom of the bag opened, a little of the Easter grass sprinkled down over her feet. She bent to pick it off the floor, her long hair almost touching it. "They're slippery," pointing to some caught between the straps of her sandals. Danny looked at her feet and delighted in the way she wiggled her big toe as she tried to free it from a couple of strands, and at the cute little one, without the strands, and at the nail polish; each toe was a different pastel. "Where'd you say you got this stuff?"

He looked up from those endearing feet and answered it fully voluntarily, casting away the answer's ridiculousness. "From the shredder, in the bins behind Loringer." He didn't shrug in the factory's direction; he didn't care that she didn't know where it was. "I sweep it up." He gazed into her face, "Because I can. I use it for packing things."

"What things do you pack?"

"My carvings." He tried to say it in a way that wouldn't tone it obscurely or with mystery.

She seemed unsure, then quickly perked, "Loringer? My step-father used to work there."

Coming back in, Roy asked, "Did you live here?"

"No, but he did. Well, used to."

Danny steered the conversation back to him, "Does he work there now?"

"No. Used to. He moved. In with my mom. That's how I heard about Gilmore"

They tried determining a timeframe; whether Danny might have known him, but decided that here step-father wasn't there when Danny started. Of course, none of that mattered; Danny would have talked about chickens had Mallorie mentioned eggs.

Then, at last, "Hey, I'm Danny Furman."

"I'm Mallorie." They held hands in a handshake-like way, but more as if trading something. Mallorie. It rhymed with eventually. That's all he needed to remember.

They spoke about where she'd transferred from, about some other things—later, Danny had forgotten what they'd said exactly, being distracted—and, *no she didn't want a cup of coffee* and, *yes, he could have her phone number* and then *okay, good-bye* and then when she had to leave, she gave him a small piece of paper with yet smaller numbers in an auricular cursive, as if written with the fine stroke a tiny feather.

Danny watched her go, her long braided hair swaying across the small of her back, her jean pockets clutching back and forth. He slipped the paper into his wallet.

"Just like that, huh," Roy encouraged. Danny slipped the tiny paper with its tinier numbers into his wallet.

Danny unfolded, then re-folded her number for a day, then went back to the campus studio. There she was. "I'm a transferring senior," she said shaking Danny's hand, again. From Gillford College, he learned. He asked where she'd been before Gillford. ("Some small place on the coast of North Carolina," Danny told Randall when he'd asked Danny if he had any girlfriends, "but I can't remember where exactly.")

"Probably a small, tiny artist's colony," he supposed.

"No," she chuckled, humored by his assumption, "it wasn't. Not an artist's colony. But, it's small."

Within a few minutes, Danny also learned that she'd been a marine biology major, then, inspired by an unknown, changed it to Fiber-Arts at Gillford. "A *large* artist's colony," giving Danny two sympathetic elbow nudges. "So, now," her arms up, palms outward, "here I am," as if by magic spell she'd suddenly materialized right in front of him.

"Yes you are."

"You should see the campus art's studio."

Which, the following day, he did.

It was a small, rough-sawn building fitted between the trees at the edge of campus, like a cabin in the woods. Filled with fabrics: cloth and felting; woven materials. Shredded, dyed, draped textiles that would stretch and wrap and swathe over wire, mesh, plaster. Seashells. Dried ocean creatures. Starfish, their rigid arms contorted as if twisted gymnasts. Long twigs of coral like the bleached bones in the osteology lab. All those bizarrely inflexible, skeletonous, unyielding things displayed inflexibly. Though, when clothed, then draped in soft fabric, and after that sculptured under affectionate care, the inflexible became softly supple with Mallorie's touch. Each was exhibited on studio shelves for public admiration; then later, privately, at home on her apartment shelves, across her kitchen counter. Alongside her bedside table.

Danny lurched down the apartment stairs and swayed onto the driveway, arms wrapped tightly around the engorged coroner bags. He set them beside the car. One slippery bag slowly tipped sideward. He shoved it upward, pushing on it so that it snugged against a tire. The bag expelled air. A handful of limey, sinuous strands puffed out through the zipper, drifted frivolously, and settled gracefully around the wheel rim. He held the bag flattened. For a reason he could not name, the day at the Dot Your Eye and Mallorie with the sandy Easter grass she'd raked out of the Sand Pool and then tersely handed to Roy came memorably. After a pause, he released the bag and watched it gradually inhale. When it returned to its former bloated size, he studied its flatness momentarily. Randall came to mind, crossly. Pushing on the bag, now harder, harder, it gasped, coughing green shreds through the half-zipped zipper. Danny pressed it further until it was all but deflated, pitilessly. Then, releasing, it rose slowly, refilling through the zipper links with a sucking wheeze not unlike that of an overweight man drawing breath at the end of a steep climb. Fully inflated, the bag returned to its original puffed-up blackness.

Captivated by the weird sputtering, hushing, strand fluttering all of his doings had made, Danny considered repeating it all over again. But didn't; the thing to do now was to fix the radio; hook it to the antenna. He walked around the car. Once again, the trunk hood had settled half-closed, agape like the mouth of a befuddled child. He raised the hood fully open; thought about propping something in it to keep it that way—but didn't. Instead, he climbed into the front seat and began to tunnel under the dashboard, returning back to the neck-throbbing, spine bending weave he'd been in when he'd decided that he'd needed to use pliers—not his fingers.

Rooting his arms behind the dashboard, digging into the wiry nest, he fingered the pliers through it until he found the wire and screw of his search. He pushed the screw that way and twisted the wire this way, turning his body so that in the end he got the wire where he thought it should be. It took some additional contorting to shove himself closer to the wires, like a burrowing owl—his fingers, talons. He hooked two wires together expecting the tick of an electric link. Nothing. Maybe, he thought, he'd pull that other thing out—whatever it was called—and it might go there. So, he tried that, hoping it'd be the radio jack. He guessed that if the green wire was the going-to wire, then the white must be the coming-from wire. Yes, the going-to wire. That's it. The simile amused him: like *going to do something.* Or, *where are you coming from?* He studied the last wire left. As he brought the wires toward each other, his last thought was, *do you suppose that'll do it?* Click....

.....*Baaaoowwh oom-bash!* The sound of the explosion was physical. It walloped his face before the impact barreled into his ears: a mill-instant rupturing, an ear- fissuring explosion. At the same time, a hideous screaming, like the gruesome wail of skidding tires, followed by a brutally riotous lung-collapsing thumping and pounding, as if a lurid tribe of drumming natives had come from beneath the dashboard.

And, along with all of that, yet again, he'd sliced his hand; the sound wave like the burn of a hot stove, jerking his hand away from it.

There was a throbbing electric bass guitar and a shrilling caw from of a lead singer that Rock N' Rolled piercingly. The brain-deadening sound punched its way out the car, spun out onto the driveway, and flared down the street like a coalmine explosion. Danny jerked as if by electrocution. His leg slipped from the door, it swung closed. It locked his ankle between the armrest and the latch, as it had while he'd struggled with the wiring, before the explosion.

Upside down between the steering wheel and front seat, trapped as if from fallen such mine debris, he kicked at the door. "Jesus Fuckin' Christ!" With unaccustomed speed he did an instant reverse corkscrew and squirmed from his contorted position. He stood, dizzied from noise, and balanced himself against the car. The singer still continued to shriek, the bass to plummet, the drums to maraud. He leaned ear-wounded into the car, wrenched the ignition key to off, and yanked it from its slot. The music attack stopped. "Holy hell!"

He glared at the steering column, at where the ignition key had been. He wondered why he had put it in that way, stupidly, and why it had been in the *ON* position. He looked across the street and wondered, too, whether Mr. Oliver Pennick had heard the tumult blast, might have interrupted his nap, brought him out. He'd come over, dazed. The porch door did not open.

Danny checked his hand. While the memory-racking music's numb grew fainter, he remembered slicing his wrist on something knife-like down there under the dashboard. He checked his hand. The bleeding stopped, he wiped the smear against the back of his pants. He juggled the car keys undecidedly. He put them on the car hood. Took a breath. Silence. Calm. He looked again at the key chain.

Not calm. *Ah, shit. The apartment key.*

It was upstairs, inside, next to his checkbook, both of them on the table that was well beyond the door that slammed well locked behind him when he'd walked out arms filled with bags of Easter grass.

Time was of the essence. Fuck, it's almost eleven o'clock. His time-math calculations figured he'd be late getting to Mallorie's house. He couldn't go and get Randall's key. That wouldn't work. He'd have to actually see him, not to mention everybody else at Loringer. He'd seen enough of Loringer and Randall for this life.

He'd break into the apartment. Without considering consequences, Danny went to his toolbox, selected a hefty screwdriver, and ran up the stairs to the locked door. With a bloodied hand cupped and to his forehead, he peered through the small window. A worn curtain obscured, but, yes, they were, still there. "Yep," Danny said to nobody.

Yep was more than just about a key. In there also was his canvas dufflebag. It stood just where he'd left it, waiting there large and full and ready, alone in the center of the kitchen, propped up patiently. Of course he knew it was there as soon as he'd seen the key-missing ring chain resting there on the car. The *ah-shit* was not at all about writing Randall a rent check, it was the locked-in-the-apartment dufflebag.

He'd left it there conspicuously, purposefully. So that in the very—*very*—unlikely event he might forget it, he wouldn't. He'd left it inside, to protect it, intentional that it'd be the very—*very*—last thing he'd put into the car. Load the important goods last. Set it on the seat like a passenger. All else was baggage, temporary chattel, stuff, inanimate things; even the rocking chair, its value only nostalgic. That duffle bag held intangible possessions—souls.

Danny shoved the screwdriver between wood trim and doorplate, separating them with an aggressive *keratching* split. *Who cares?* He'll be gone soon and then it'll be Randall's problem. He went into the kitchen, took the key, slid it into his pocket. He cinched the dufflebag strings tight, and hefted it over his shoulder.

Leaving the apartment he pushed the door open too widely, and then when turning around to close it, knocked a plant-less vase off the porch railing. The vase bounced once, then still intact, went airborne until at last it shattered on the sidewalk below. A worthless piece of junk that Randall said had value. Danny shoved the door, pushed it harder. Booted it snug. Grumping, he clumped down the stairs. At the bottom, he kicked the vase shards. They seemed to be in satisfactory pieces. He huffed out to the driveway but stopped huffing when he reached his strewn belongings. He stood quiet among them like a bewildered homeowner after the hurricane, standing in the wet dawn, surveying the aftermath.

Where to begin the sorting, the directionless sifting? The antenna now fixed, it was time to pack the car. As planned. Danny did a selective inventory: too much stuff, not enough time. He considered getting rid of some of it. Leave it behind. But he couldn't and knew he wouldn't. Although, just moments ago it'd all been simply worthless stuff. The dufflebag was getting burdensome hanging there over his shoulder. Gosh, it struck him heavily, he was a migratory compulsive. More than once he'd said to Mallorie, "People should be more like nomads. Able to gather up all they own at a moment's notice, load it, and move on. Like bohemian ascetics. No possessions." But he didn't follow that proclamation, he stayed put, stored his possessions for use later, like a scrub jay. His settling down and keeping around, Danny assumed, pleased Mallorie and he hoped those inclinations reassured her. He liked pleasing her. But, even the scrub jay takes off when the mood strikes.

Weary with dufflebag weight, he considered an appropriate spot for it. He chose one of the lawn chairs. He sighed and placed the bag gently, as if it was another passenger waiting. He bent over the bag, repositioned it safely. There was a woody rattle as the contents knocked against each other like a child's sack of wooden blocks. He resituated it carefully, balancing it just right, not to fall over, bent over it as if helping an elderly person get comfortable in a chair. Would you like anything else? A blanket for your knees? Danny straightened up, fixed the cinch string presentable.

There were some wood shavings caught in the pleats. He dusted them away. He guessed they came from the door, stuck to bag as he carried it out. But, maybe not? He was almost sure thought that he'd wiped everything clean before putting them all inside the duffle bag. Sometimes wood particles stick and he didn't notice.

He admired it; such a handsome sack in which to put his prideful collection. He considered the stock. *How many are there now*? Maybe a couple of dozen? He'd kidded himself. Actually, he knew exactly how many: thirty-three. Yes, thirty-three, watchfully counted, like a hen her chicks, snuggling them into the nest with care.

But that's only part of it. The rest of it, the half of it, the other share to be determined later. With hopes, many will soon be displayed somewhere. Could he put them out for sale? Would someone buy them? Before he'd packed them away, Danny considered giving a few away. He was sure that they had a valuable tender. Maybe one to Marty, over at Snuggies; he might still owe Marty a couple beers. They were worth more than that, but Marty had said he'd like one someday, "before they get expensive," he'd kidded. For sure, absolutely none to Randall.

There were a few, the special ones, which he kept reserved especially for himself, a narcissistic pledge of his fidelity to his craft. After all, he wanted to retain one thing in life as a tangible symbol of how he'd be defined. That thing was his collection. Even if it apologetic, it was his.

With some penitence, though. A number of those special ones lingered insecurely in a dark place where selflessness cowered. A devil there said to Danny that his carvings were not accomplished   Something here about Danny's insecurity about how good his carvings are?

Everything else was for Mallorie; even his forlorn misgivings. Mallorie so faraway; Mallorie so near. Pensively he swept the last tiny wood chips off the dufflebag. Looked about. He wished knew in which of all those boxes was her photograph; it would be as if she were there in soul.

Now Danny fretted. He felt pressed, like one of the inhaling and exhaling bags he'd squeezed. He straightened the handle on the duffle bag. The sound of a truck motor made him look up. The mail truck passed, slowed, then continued. That meant that time would quicken. He carried two boxes to the back of the car. The trunk hood was half-closed. *Get started* he huffed silently, pushing the hood upward once more.

Danny has had more starts than a derby horse. He has never won a purse, placed anything, or shown any money. Yet somehow his odds stay low. He's assured that the pay-off is coming. He thinks that if he runs enough races sooner or later they'll take his picture while standing in the winner's circle.

"If you run with the best, you're bound to win," Randall once said. Or, perhaps twice. Or, maybe even six time in direct ratio to the finished beers. Randall: the speaker of clichés, the practitioner of none.

Sure, Danny's run with the best, yet he still has to come in neck-to-neck with any of them. In high school his best friend was valedictorian—where Danny graduated with mediocre grades. During college, Danny roomed with some Greensburg University students. While they studied he took community college classes. Long after they'd graduated, he was still in school. He was friends with a local rock band, and while they performed he stood along stage playing the tambourine. Carried the equipment. Untangled microphones. A few years later, and still not graduated, he lived with a girlfriend. They did laundry together. He moved out after she started bringing in matched pillow cases, placemats, his favorite toothpaste.

Danny lifted the trunk hood higher. He stood with his foot on the bumper. He looked over the car roof for the mail truck. Then, as if a starter's whistle had blown, he dashed among the things making a frantic triage of the scattered. He reached for the first box handiest, put it into the trunk, glanced across the street again. No sign of Mr. Oliver Pennick. Not yet. And, with any luck, not today.

But he might. Daily, Mr. Oliver Pennick's emergence followed when the mail truck passed. Typically, he'll appear wearing a loosened button-up sweater, a flannel shirt tucked insecurely. He'll stand determinedly in a pair of voluminous trousers that drape around his gangly legs like a tent collapsed on its poles. He'll toddle out on the porch—sometimes in pajamas—and check that the mail truck has passed. Tugging and shifting inside his loose clothing as if crawling from that tent he'll go out for his mail. If it looked like he saw Danny, he'd wave at him. After which he'll climb back up on the porch, close the door, and go inside.

Back when Mr. Oliver Pennick was Danny's new neighbor—new to Danny, not to the neighborhood or Mr. Oliver Pennick—Danny would watch stealthily for any Mr. Oliver Pennick activity. Although, when sighted, he'd bow to him, politely hiding his disgust. Not Mr. Oliver Pennick's disgust, Danny's disgust.

Danny picked up another box, carried it to the car. He imagined Mr. Oliver Pennick over there across the street, in his house, not yet getting his mail. He could almost hear Mr. Oliver Pennick calling from his mailbox, "How are you on this fine day Daniel Furman?" Sure, Danny would wave. Maybe even bow. Those things were something he's begun doing early in their neighborliness. (Or, as will be after this day...*did*.) It was around that time that Danny began addressing Oliver Pennick as *Mr. Oliver Pennick* with such properness.

It was the Saturday following the first week of Danny as Randall's roommate Mr. Oliver Pennick came across the street to meet Danny. Prior to that day, their sightings were from across their respective walkways; and only sighted if Danny was between his apartment and the car. That day, Mr. Oliver Pennick called across, "How are you today?" Standing next to his mailbox, balancing wobbly, he raised a fistful of envelopes, "It's a good day for mail." The gestures were clearly an offer to meet but Danny did not respond. He was getting ready to drive out to the campus and see Mallorie's studio. He was just about to open the car door when he looked out and saw his not yet named elderly neighbor coming across the street.

He had an unhurried determination, as if the street crossing were to step across a stream, not to slip on the rocks. Danny stood at the car, behind the opened door, a hand on the steering wheel; a key dangled from his finger. Mr. Oliver Pennick raised his arm, giving Danny the impression that perhaps he wanted a ride, that maybe Danny was a taxi driver.

Mr. Oliver Pennick sauntered, watching each footstep for a stumbling thing, but pressed diligently onward. Danny bent, checked the seat that his present for Mallorie was on it, pretended arranging. There were no sidewalks in that neighborhood; only driveways. Danny stole a look over the dashboard. Mr. Oliver Pennick paused where Danny's driveway started. Danny rolled up the window. Mr. Oliver Pennick took three steps but at the beginning of the driveway he leaned and picked something up off the ground. Straightening, he looked leftward, down the street, as if whatever he'd found might belong to someone down there. He put the thing into a pocket on his button-up sweater. Buttoned it closed. He looked up the street rightward, scratched behind his ear, and stared for a moment. Danny hoped that Mr. Oliver Pennick would walk there, return whatever it was to whoever had lost it, and turn around. Instead, he faced Danny and came toward him straightaway, tottering up the driveway now with some speed, then halfway, stopped abruptly and held one hand out that seemed to stretch for a railing that wasn't there. Resting, he reached inside the button-up sweater pocket with the other hand and unbuttoned it. Perhaps, Danny guessed, for recollection.

 Danny closed the car door, stepped forward, and letting his arms drop slackly which suddenly made him feel as if he was back in high school and Mr. Letterstock was coming up to ask Danny where his hall pass was.

"Danny Furman." He'd said flatly after Mr. Oliver Pennick had asked. Shaking hands, Danny speculated that somewhere in the past there might have been a larger, more healthful, Mr. Oliver Pennick contained inside that sagged clothing. "So, Daniel Furman," glancing upward at the apartment, "So, now you are my new neighbor." Danny didn't know if it was declarative, or interrogative; still reminiscent of Mr. Letterstock. Then, shifting, hand on a hip, he looked at Danny, "I see there where you have moved in with that Randall."

*That Mr. Randall...*Jesus, right off the bat! As in: *that Randall* from work? Like some mocking thing someone might say about him there? "Did you hear what that Randall...." and then off they'd go, reeling about some ridiculous thing that Randall had done.

Mr. Oliver Pennick adjusted his sweater pocket button, "That Randall likes to stay to himself, does he not?" Danny heard a tone in the question that seemed to convey doubt. Doubt about choosing *that Randall* as a roommate. Was it a leading question? Did this long-limbed neighbor have reservations concerning the wisdom someone possessed who'd move in with Randall? Was Mr. Oliver Pennick suspicious? Danny didn't know what to say, so, he said: "Yeah." Then, using an inflection that would verify prudence, show he'd gotten to know Randall, assert his judgment, he declared "a couple of weeks ago." Danny found himself looking up at the window also. "Yeah, that's like him." Quickly, he felt a need to clarify further that he'd known Randall for longer than just two weeks; that he'd come prepared. "Me and Randall work together at Loringer's."

Mr. Oliver Pennick looked up at the apartment window again; perhaps to know if Randall might be there. Danny found that he was looking up at the window with Mr. Oliver Pennick. "Yeah, that's like him." *That Randall?*

Mr. Oliver Pennick arched, stretched, and folded his arms together in the way an older carpenter collapses a wood folding rule. "It has been very pleasant to meet you Daniel Furman, but I must be going home." He ambled back the way he'd come, watching for the stumbling things again, but crossing the street with less caution, now that he seemed to know his way.

And that's the way it began on that first opening day: *"I'm very pleased to meet you, Daniel Furman,"* always using first and last name with formal rhythm. "Don't you think it's a pleasant day, Daniel Furman?" And that's the way it was. And the way it would also be for Danny; that on that day this proper neighbor would become Mr. Oliver Pennick.

And then there were those other days too, days when Mr. Oliver Pennick would catch Danny getting into his car and Mr. Oliver Pennick, drawing his hand over the hood, would ask, "How is this car of yours running , Daniel Furman?" Danny would snap his fingers, then point one back at Mr. Pennick, winking, "It's runnin' real good, Mr. Oliver Pennick," adding in a jerky staccato, sarcastically, "yep, tip-top shape." He thought about making a brash remark about the similarity of older cars and Mr. Oliver Pennick, but refrained civilly, not knowing him so well yet. He did, however, attempt flattery. "You're runnin' in tip-top shape too, Mr. Oliver Pennick." Danny figured Mr. Pennick to be over seventy—or maybe eighty-something. He couldn't say. Nor did he know how long he'd been in this neighborhood. It was Danny's guess that Mr. Oliver Pennick has probably been living in that same house, on this same street, and getting his mail from the same mailbox forever. That's what Danny guessed.

"You're terrible at guessing ages," Mallorie chided kindly.

"Especially girls," Randall chided not kindly, reminding Danny pitilessly of the night they were waiting for Laura—the girlfriend with the placemats and toothpaste— at Snuggies for beers. Advocated that Laura was well old enough to drink there. "She's twenty-four," he assured

Randall. When Laura showed the bartender her ID, he handed it back demurely. Randall snatched it from her fingers, read it. "Not even fuckin' close, Danny." He gave Danny a heckling shoulder-shake, slapped the bar, "Good fuckin' call ump!"

Even if Mr. Oliver Pennick was indeed eighty-something, it didn't matter. What mattered to Danny was that Mr. Oliver Pennick had stayed fixed in one place for so long. "Thirty-six years," Mr. Oliver Pennick had boasted to Danny, even though Danny hadn't asked. Said then, it was a dubious boast, closing in on detestable when he thought about such a confining duration. He imagined a bird in a cage.

Though at the same time, he admired it because throughout all of that there must have been consistency: changes in the neighborhood, time passing uniformly, the comings and goings. Conceding acceptance toward stability, a place there always to come back to, he considered a homing pigeon.

Danny accepted Mr. Oliver Pennick's visits conveniently; it seemed they came at a time when he was either going to, or coming from, both within a limited schedule. Many, annoyingly, were too extended and were often followed by some cautionary admonition from Mr. Oliver Pennick. The time Danny cracked the side mirror on his car. "You need to take care when backing up," Mr. Oliver Pennick advised, peering into it as if a magnifying glass. Danny hatless, coatless, black rain clouds forming, "I believe, Danny Furman, that you'll need a good skimmer and a mackintosh today." The morning after one of Randall's midnight motorcycle blast-offs, the muffler and exhaust a fireworks cannonade. "I'm afraid that that Randall takes a wild hair sometimes, don't you agree Danny Furman?"

Danny Furman did. "Yeah, Mr. Pennick, he gets set off that way."

"I'm terribly concerned. I'd say that that motorcycle sounds awfully unsafe to me."

"Well, that's just the way Randall is. I say, live and let live. You know?"

Mr. Oliver Pennick tucked his mail meditatively chestwise, as if a preacher his bible. "If that Mr. Randall persists to ride in such a hazardous manner, he won't live to let it."

Mr. Oliver Pennick's opinions concluded summarily with a rendering of judgment: On drink: "It is not a safe thing to do. Drinking beer and riding a motorcycle." On work: "Your dreams don't come around by magic; it takes a great deal of sweat and determination." On the postal service: "It seems to me that that post truck driver could get here on a more dependable schedule." Impatiently, Danny heard those opinions as them of a conformant curmudgeon; yet he allowed tolerance, agreeing that the suggestion that it wasn't magic; that sweat and determination was meaningful.

Danny even rehearsed Mr. Oliver Pennick greetings, *Hello, Mr. Pennick. Ya out for a walk? Hi, Mr. Pennick. How are you today?* practicing them with proscribed deliberation, careful diction. enunciating each option twice, changing the inflection, attempting polite patience, the way Mr. Oliver Pennick did.

Every now and then it occurred to Danny —usually admitted by the time Mr. Oliver Pennick was halfway across the street—that there were times when he'd offered a few particles of uncomplicated, innocent insight, as if his elder neighbor was almost father-like in delivering guidance; Danny, son-like. In moments such as those—the insinuations about Randall—Danny became in a manner like he was Randall's younger brother; even needing to cover foibles, "Something sometimes he just does." On one occasion an appreciative impulse flashed, although Danny did not say it: "Yes, sir."

About Mallorie: "How's that pretty young woman I've seen you with? She appeared to be well turned-out. I don't mean it an improper way."

Such were the questions. The uncannily timed stopovers seemed to pry the way a father would meddle; often oblivious to intimate matters. Then, from Danny, an unsaid *mind-your-own-business*. "She's very nice," evasively. He did not tell him about Mallorie; certainly not then, on the last day of neighborliness.

She'd waved at him a few times—getting in and out of the car; going up to Danny's apartment. And she wouldn't be coming over here any longer, refusing vehemently to shun Randall. She'd nick-named him *Rancid*, spitefully.

"You seem kind on her. I reckon you're a sweet couple."

Danny shied from going further with that. He protecting his space, her space, ignoring the possibility of Mr. Oliver Pennick's voyeurism. Using his word, "Yeah, she's definitely sweet."

"I'd say that by now you two were terrifically close. Is that not right?"

And so on and that sort of thing. It was that kind of Mr. Oliver Pennick, the one with too many questions, the inquisitive neighbor, he was the one that Danny didn't want to see coming over here now, not while he was trying to pack, getting ready to see Mallorie, loading the dufflebag. Those being that Danny suspected him following the goings on, then dragging himself across the street to inquire about them; comment on them. Danny supposed that Mr. Oliver Pennick might be over there in his house, waiting for the mail, looking to see what was up, was a suppose that Danny didn't like that came around too frequently.

Even then, on that important day, the day of parting, parting he could be was there watching. Indifferent to it for the moment, Danny dragged a lawn chair to the car, dropped the box of comic books behind the passenger seat, raised the trunk hood higher, and studied the space in it for more. He fetched another jumbled boxful; glancing cautiously across the street he put the box into the trunk.

Mr. Oliver Pennick's assertion, *I'd say that by now you two were terrifically close* came back to Danny in the same manner he'd been going about remembering what he had to pack in the car, unpredictably. Of course they were close. Even sweet; terrifically. What had it been now? Seven months? He revealed personal things. That was close, wasn't it? That chilly evening in her studio—Mallorie insulated inside a wool blanket, crouched over a simmering pot of decoupage and when Danny came in and hugged her, the blanket became as if a sheath of fire welding them. It did not take long until they shared inward things outwardly.

But not right away. He had not shown all quite yet.

He was still just Danny Furman, self-apologetically, sometimes in, and sometimes out—nevertheless, always trying to get closer to the center. So far, he'd exposed only the top part, making him like a headshot; someone seen only from the shoulders up, the rest of him not shown in the photo. It made him feel as if he were one of his own carvings; not all of him there. At the same time, he experienced a whirling inwardness that he knew, and why he knew it, he couldn't put a word to, that hadn't been fully released, but that spun like the wheel inside a spiraling gyro toy did when pulled.

Danny was wholly grateful that she was appreciative. He believed that because she is an artist, she can understand the concept that something can have more than appears, that needing more is not a sign of incompletion. Mallorie said that Danny's partial workmanship didn't mean something unfinished. She disclosed to Danny that she didn't know why exactly, but she was content with the way they were. *They*...his talents. And, *they*...them. He loved that.

"There's always more," delicately putting another back into his dufflebag, "creativity has no ending."

So, *yes,* he whispered as he humped his laundry sack to the car and dropped it into a space where there had been a spare tire.

And there was more: spread uncollected around the driveway. He gathered some. He layered the cardboard posters, his jumbled magazines, and the tattered atlas on top of the other stuff as if making a lasagna casserole. Then, Mallorie's sketchbooks. He glanced cautiously for any sign of Mr. Oliver Pennick.

There were days when he'd *not* glanced cautiously and here came Mr. Oliver Pennick. Like that Wednesday when Danny had to be at work—why he can remember that it was a Wednesday, evades him—when Mr. Oliver Pennick appeared, navigating the street diagonally, as if it was a chessboard and he was determining which were the black or red squares. He looked each way, advanced unwaveringly toward Danny.

Danny huffed; bad timing. He was already late for third-shift and not particularly in an advice-receiving mood.

Mr. Oliver Pennick trudged up the drive, one shoe too loose. He slid it to keep it tight on his foot, a slight lift, then a leathery swoosh. *Lift and swoosh, lift and swoosh,* until he came to the car and stood elderly. He leaned against Danny's car, winded from his street-crossing journey. Bending over he slipped a finger into his shoe, aligned around his heel. A loose sweater drooped, jumbling the faded red-diamond patterns. The collarless shirt under the sweater was curiously well-pressed. His belted suspenders stretched over his boney shoulders like taut strapping around kindling. His pants looked as if they belonged to a stilt-walker; the slack in them coiled around his ankles like rope needing winding. A wadded lump of something protruded from a pant pocket.

Perhaps envelopes, Danny guessed as he got out of the car for Mr. Oliver Pennick. Danny did not meet his eyes, instead looked at Mr. Oliver Pennick's shoes. They seemed dog-chewed, but no dog had ever been seen; at least none that barked. Mr. Oliver Pennick scratched at his hip, rubbed his thigh and the way he did it further aggravated Danny's impression of him as an old-man, and that whatever he'd stuffed into his pocket wouldn't be pulled out and blown into. Because Danny was now getting yet later for work, his impatient mood exacerbated higher, growing with disgust that Mr. Oliver Pennick had chosen now to stop by. His hygiene of the day, his clumsily postured shifting, pocket fussing, and car leaning at this moment fostered intolerance, not neighborliness.

After a few steps, he came around to where Danny stood waiting. Clasping at the door frame for balance, he asked, "Looks like you are getting ready for work Daniel Furman."

"I am." There, much too close was Mr. Oliver Pennick breathing, the snapping sound of his fingernails on the window gasket, the shuffle of his shoes, the breathy presence of maturity.

"Well, if you weren't, maybe you should get out in the day. I think it's going to be a dry one," he continued, leaning even closer. "Cool. No rain."

Danny hunched, unlistening. He feigned an interest in weather forecast. *Go away*, an inner voice said rudely. Finally, "Hey, you know, I do have to go to work."

"That's unfortunate. A job can be a distraction."

That was exactly what Danny needed—a distraction. For that, he looked at the inspection sticker on the windshield. There was a lengthy, hook-shaped scratch above. No longer needing to pretend distraction, Danny rubbed at the mark.

"Ah, fuck!" Mr. Pennick startled backward. Danny rubbed the mark. A slurry of Randall's motorcycle tires came to mind. Then, quickly, the neighbor standing near, "Sorry."

"Accepted. But you should watch your language. I can tell that upsets you, but it shouldn't be a cause for cursing."

Danny picked at the mark, trying to make the reprimand and the scratch go away. Rubbing, "Will this make it disappear?"

Mr. Pennick inspected. "Car glass gets nicked all the time." He rubbed. "I used to polish them out with denture cream." He smiled. He looked at Danny as if at picture taking was next.

It was then that Danny became aware how near they were. He'd always seen Mr. Oliver Pennick at a distance, relatively; never this close. A set of perfectly aligned teeth brimmed dazzlingly. They were impeccable with a luridly translucent, milk-glass whiting.

As if to acknowledge Danny's attentive study, lips spread apart proudly, molars like trophies, gums—synthetic, pinkly opaque—clean and plastic were held wide open by thumb and fingers. "Works on teeth, too." He wiggled his lips, "See!"

Indeed, he did see. He saw teeth that looked incompatible, obvious, like a differently colored car door replaced because of a collision. Too glossy and out of place. Then Mr. Pennick showed Danny the other side. "Shines all of them like polished silver." White uniformed parade marchers on a pink ballfield came to mind. He didn't know whether to compliment, or flinch. He chose compliment. It came out, although, struggled and awkward. "Those look like good teeth." He cocked his head for scrutiny, then obtusely, looking closer, "They seem like they'd be good to eat with." As soon as it'd come out, he wished he hadn't said it;

just another one of his simpleton's remarks. *Jesus, what else would you do with teeth?* It was something a stupid little kid would've said.

"Yes. They sure are." Mr. Pennick slipped his fingers away, grazed them on his sweater. He worked his jaw up and down as if to readjust the denture fit, making a puppy chewing on a toy motion. "And they are not cheap. If you don't take care of your teeth now, you will find that you have ones like these in your mouth."

Danny was unaware that he was involuntarily pressing his cheeks, rubbing at his mouth with his knuckles, and slipping his tongue around teeth he couldn't remember brushing before he'd gotten ready for work, stopping abruptly when he felt Mr. Oliver Pennick straining nearer, closer to Danny's head. "What?" Mortified, Danny turned quickly, and reaching self-consciously for the car door handle. "I think that's enough of this." What was next? Flossing? "Don't you worry, Mr. Oliver Pennick, I brush them all the time. And watch what I eat."

"I don't have to brush my teeth," clicking them, stretching his jaw.

"I see that."

Closing his mouth, "You should avoid sweets."

Danny wanted to shout, *Holy Christ! You ain't my dad? I'll take care of my own fucking teeth.* Instead, pulling the door open, making a going-to-get-in sign, he politely excused, "Okay," punctuating closure, "I still need to get to work; like today."

"And floss. Do you floss?"

That was it. "Stop it!" He'd shouted. Then, immediately apologetic, "I gotta tell you, I don't have time to talk about dentistry." Ratting car keys, "I gotta get to work." He looked over the top of the car door at Mr. Oliver Pennick standing like an impediment behind it, "Today."

"That's okay. Don't mind me. I get sidetracked." Mr. Oliver Pennick wiped his face, pulled the wad out of his pocket, blew.

Danny shut the door. "Goodbye." Backing out of the driveway the reflection of Mr. Oliver Pennick appeared distantly in the sideview mirror—the still cracked one. He was crossing the street; probably to check in on his mailbox.

Danny fitted another knick-knack filled box geometrically, squarely fixing it between wheel-well and trunk hinges—the freely moveable ones that did not hold the trunk open the way they should. He picked what had been under there first and there, wrapped solicitously, was Mallorie's photograph. No, he was awfully relieved; it hadn't gotten misplaced, the way he'd been so worried about.

In it, Mallorie's raven hair has the sheered phosphorescence like the feathers of that fascinating bird. Her long tress, tied in a yarn-yoked ponytail cascades to her hips. Or, as the image of her comes finer, curled in a French roll, or looped like a scarf while sleeping. He imagines rolling her black locks between his fingers, the glimmering strands. Now she's there lounging in the bathtub, her hair a long black stole floating above her breasts; suds like surf beaching at her hips. Her soap-covered legs, rising and then submerging, are slender and white and supple, bringing to mind—childishly, he consents—velvety pipe cleaners. Her arms emerge, the ones that will flex equally around a grocery bag, a pillow—his chest. He pictures her face, invitingly it becomes a porcelain dinner plate: her eyes, nose, lips set daintily like delicious appetizers. *Just little nibbles, please* he murmured quietly to no one.

His first intimate adulations he'd said to her lumbered awkwardly, and without speed. Their intimacy came ineptly, and without speed. In those early introductory days, she made him feel gawky, like a seagull hobbling upon some shiny beach thing, unidentified until he got close and tapped on it. Mallorie accepted his klutziness by letting him shred fabrics, shake paint. It took several weeks for Danny to be at ease with her automatic dancing. After that, things between them were more spontaneous.

He put the box that stored her photograph into place in the trunk reserved for its special attention. Her reflection lingered. In the picture she wears a sallow gown, more like a gauzy robe, but under it he imagines her breasts, small nectarine-shaped spheres, un-subdued. She poses as if to dance, which out of the picture, in the real, she does impulsively; twirling as if taffy, spinning out the candy scent of strawberry—creamy vanilla if such a creamy texture could have an aroma. What was the motive for her spontaneous dancing? Just like most of all she did, without announcement. Just like many of her motives, unnecessary.

Of course Danny adored it when she danced, but as an uneasy flatterer, he'd said it clumsily. "You dance like a canary in a birdbath."

Spontaneous birdbath dancing came much later in the course of their growing friendship. It took Danny four days of unfolding and re-folding the tiny slip of paper Mallorie had given him that day at the Dot Your Eye until he was ready to call her on his cell phone; the intermittent one, the one whose battery indicator was always shriveled emptily.

After he'd asked, she said, "Yes." After she asked, he said, "something in black-and-white." To which he said, "On campus" after she asked, "Where?" After the movie—they both agreed the story was awkward; the gags embarrassing—they got into his car and drove out to a party thrown by some of Danny's newly made friends. Friends whose house he was unsure of where it was.

Driving through the campus gate Mallorie looked behind at the backseat, "So, what's with the big canvas bag?"

At that time, Danny didn't know if she was being curious or sly. Before he'd asked her out, back at the Dot Your Eye, during the movie, and now on the road to the party, Danny had erroneously presumed that somehow Mallorie might have heard enough about him that he didn't need to unveil such things with full explanation. After all, a lot of what they did was gossip about each other. Surely, he reflected, someone must have said something about what he'd had in that bag.

Randall knew. Or, acted like he knew, or tried to show he understood. But, more often, all he showed was just cruel indulgence. Too many evenings, Randall would slip behind Danny while he worked at his table, and Randall would pick up a wood chunk, roll it around in his hand as if palming a baseball, taunt critically about the wood carving, and remark derisively about its formlessness; its weird eyes, its unfamiliar shape, jeering. "You figure you can really sell these fuckin' things?" He plunked it on the table. "It looks like a dinosaur a goddamn two-year old would make." Danny is clear about one particular night—recalling it with irritating clarity for Mallorie.

Mallorie faced Danny, but Danny did not have to see her to sense someone uncomfortable was facing him. After a moment, she rested her arm across the seat, her hand not far from Danny's shoulder. Perhaps, changing his sense, she was getting relaxed. "So," she said, lifting her arm, waving her hand behind Danny's head. She gestured her head toward the rear seat as if she were speaking to someone back there instead, "Are you going to keep what's back there a secret?"

That time he heard how she'd asked in a different ear, perceived a unfriendly tone. Her tone made him feel stupidly self-conscious. He tried an evasive preface, "It's got my stuff in it. Tools." He glanced up at the rearview mirror, the dufflebag reflection shaded in the darkness about. He raised his eyebrows, feigned theatrical, trying to be mysterious, but also charming. "And things I can't show you." He rumpled his brow. "At least not right now. Maybe later."

No longer waving, arm off the seat near him, "When is later?"

He searched for the road as he thought he'd been told where to search. He slowed the car. "It's kinda personal."

"Oh." Hands into her lap, folded. "I see." She looked out the side window.

A road appeared. Danny turned for it. A fraternity house emerged between gnarled trees.

Mallorie looked up at the branches as they passed beneath. "Something personal?"

Danny steered onto the road. He felt adrift, and began to think that being lost here on this road wasn't the only thing that was going adrift. He put his arm where Mallorie had had hers. "Not like that kind of personal."

"Oh?" She rotated his direction. "Now that you have me way out here near nowhere alone…"

An obscurely lighted house appeared, but at it a party was clearly underway: torches around the trees, a keg on the porch, dark figures writhing in the flame lighted shadows behind the trees, a wide-open door, bright light and loud music from it. Now closer, Danny recognized it for a fraternity house; some of the guys familiar from campus pumping at the beer nozzle.

Mallorie leaned forward. "Are we going there?"

Danny stopped the car, bent forward, and peered through the windshield around Mallorie. "Oh, God no. Not that place." He started up the road, past all that he did not recognize. "The party's out here somewhere."

"Good."

"Yeah." The name of the road popped into mind. "The Hannon Road." The frat party now behind in the dark wake. "It's a private place."

Mallorie pivoted away from the window. She slumped backward against the seat, sighed. "Yeah, that's good." A foot on the dashboard, "At least not there." Without looking behind her, she thumbed over her shoulder indicating as Danny knew she would again, at the mass arranged so fastidiously back there. "So, what *is* in the bag?"

Again, Danny assumed she knew. He still didn't know whether she was being curious or sly. So, he thought he'd mix them up, keep the unsaid a mystery. He went with sly. "Just the heads," saying it with a casual, detached tone purposefully. He thought he'd expand the pretending. "And my sharp instruments. Sharp knives. Some saws." He stared straight ahead, trying to hide a grin, trusting she got the joke, that of course she knew there couldn't be such things in that bag. "I'll show you them later."

Mallorie "Just heads?" She looked the window at a dark house, just one window lighted. "No body?"

Danny thought she was playing along. He'd see if he could mix the story some more. "Yep. Their bodies are up here off the road in the woods."

She remained seated straightway, turning only her head toward him, blinked. Her expression took on the look of an owl watching for something to move. "Whose?"

He met her stare. Her eyes declaring clearly that she'd misheard any tone of funniness. Quickly, it occurred to him how ludicrous the conversation was going. He'd botched it. His offhanded answer, *just heads*, had meant to be cryptic, making it sound perverted, secretively comedic. Now it all sounded like it was indeed all that, and perhaps more, that it was none of her business. Did she believe he actually had something terribly creepy back there? "Oh gosh, not those kinds of heads," apologizing lamely. He didn't know whether to put his hand on her knee. "I'm sorry" He changed his mind, placed his hand on her knee. "I was being funny. Somehow I figured you already knew what's in the bag. That you knew about it; about me?"

She slid his hand away, down on the seat next to her. "I think I do now."

He drove the last part of the road to the party asking for her forgiveness about his silly humor, explaining falteringly what it was all about, the joke. He tried to justify things, earn some credibility that seemed to be falling away like the road behind them.

It seemed to help; now she was leaning closer to him, less anxiously perched on the car seat. He had just begun to account for what he had in the dufflebag, what it meant to him, when they arrived at the party house. They got out; the part about heads, unfinished.

There were a few Sand Pool people there along with some unknowns. Mallorie found an unoccupied sofa, and they sat together on it drinking a beer, then passing a joint that had appeared. Ordinarily, Danny did not drink. He smoked pot even less. Beer inflated him; pot made him feel klutzy. Stoned now, he pulled anxiously at his shirt; it looked too pink to him. He'd worn it to match his hair, to have Mallorie notice the rusty-red color. On that night, however, the marijuana and beer neither inflated him, nor klutzed him. It loosened him. Loose enough to finish what he'd been trying to explain back there in the car.

Mallorie loosened him, too. Her penetrating allure enabled him to bring out for her a picture of him that he did not usually show so readily. Keyed to impress her with his art-like perceptions, he waxed obscure, saying that his work largely unfinished yet was finished, but not in whole. He motioned to where they'd parked the car, "They're peculiar." He put his arm nearer to her shoulder. "But, they are just heads".

"So are you...peculiar." She sat lotus-like on the sofa, leaning into the cushion, bending nearer to Danny, her back to party's clamor, facing Danny. When she told him about her own pursuit, how she was really trying hard at it, Danny moved closer, too. He tried to hear her quiet voice, but with the party roaring behind them, it was like trying to listen for a particular trickle that dripped over a special rock, while around it, the louder waterfall inundated. He said they should go outside—where it was quiet. They grabbed a half-empty bottle of wine, and on the way out Mallorie joked, saying she'd been nervous, that when she saw that party down the road, she thought she was being taken to a frat party. "Frat boys are insipid," she said walking to the door. "All they want to do was take a girl upstairs." At the door she winked, "Or, outside." She laughed, poking at Danny, suggesting that here she was, indeed being taken outside. When outside, they joked about being back there in the car; how funny it was about the bag of heads misunderstanding.

It was late spring, warmer than usual. The dew-wetted lawn had not yet been mown. The high grass dampened his shoes and tickled his sockless ankles. Mallorie tiptoed, balancing on slackly strapped sandals, the wine bottle for ballast. They went to Danny's car. Mallorie took a sip of the wine, offered some to Danny. He took it, drank some. They leaned together against the car. She set the wine bottle on the car roof. She took off her sandals. She set them next to the bottle and danced a barefooted jig. "The grass is great. It feels *slip-ey* and *slide-y*. Kinda like that fake grass of yours."

Propped drowsily against Danny's car she sighed, "I need something to hold on to." Danny's elbow. "Whew...too much wine."

"You okay?"

"Tipsy"

Unable to say something supportive, he leaned beside of something helpful to say he lean Awkward Danny stare swallow-tailed jacket opened around her waist and the sleeves rolled to her elbows, sliding loosely off her arms. He gazed at her translucent silver-grey blouse, the dark, curved outline of her bra shadowed underneath it like a secret parenthesis.

Mallorie caught his fix, "Your hair looks extra red tonight. I think it's blushing."

Unhurriedly, leaning toward her, he reached around and provocatively opened the car door. He crawled into the back.

Mallorie loosed a burpy giggle. "Now what?"

Sprawled across the back seat, arms around his dufflebag, he invited, "Here, I'll show you." Pulling at the drawstrings, loosening the flaps, he opened his dufflebag.

Here now, months later, was Danny shoving box and crate across that very same backseat. He crowded them haphazardly, the way a teenage grocery-packer crams things. The dish rack with its loose pots and pans—their clacking disarray greatly taxing his attempt at order—was simply dumped. Danny went to the lawn chair with the dufflebag in it and moved the chair a bit closer to the car. He dropped the box of comic books behind the passenger seat. He studied the space for more boxes, fetched another box. As he placed that one, the mail truck returned. It stopped across from Mr. Oliver Pennick's house, the driver got out and distributed letters, and then he climbed back into the truck, waved and drove away.

He neck straightened, stretching wrangle of radio fixing out; still feeling like a mop needing wrung. A faint hum in the ears, too. The radio blast lingered. A fleeting He inspected what was left to go over there on that side of the car. Four items, or so.

Actually five if he counted the dufflebag as an item; but, it wasn't just an *item*. It was a passenger.

After some frustrated arranging Danny fit the chairs. The Easter grass would fit snuggly on either side of the chairs, nesting it all together comfy. He grabbed two bags. Synthetically lawn clippings trailed. He pushed the shred-filled balloons around the rocker. A splinter from the wicker sliced one of the bags. Green slivers puffed throughout. *Shit.* He swept at them. Fluffed like hay. He reached for the trunk hood, looked around it. Mr. Oliver Pennick was coming. Danny didn't want to say goodbye, didn't know how to.

Danny stretched, grabbed the trunk hood, made a quick look around, and slammed it closed with a solid wallop.

The sound roused memories: the ancient freezer in the basement of his mother's house that when he was there last, still closed with an ominous thud. It stands in a dark corner under the stairs, weeping condensation, full of its vague frosted shapes, arctic spikes, iced swathing, and the each summer's crystallized peaches. The enormous chrome handle, more like the lever of an enormous vault than the handhold of a rusting appliance. During insufferable summer days, Danny, not quite twelve yet, would sneak down into the basement and stand before the open door, barefooted, cooling his shirtless chest, until his mother scolded down, "Danny, close that door and get up here right away. And make sure you push it tight. It doesn't seal good." Followed by, as if she could read his mind, she'd holler, "And don't take anything out."

Growing up, it seemed like his mother used the freezer as a permanent crypt instead of temporary storage. Even now, Danny wonders if that mysterious crescent-shaped foiled bundle that his mother told him not to disturb might still be in there, undisturbed. The rime caked package never unused, likely to remain so eons into the future. Discovered by anthropologists. He did not want to be like his mother, keeping things frozen for the only reason that they could be and that maybe someday they'd have some use. That in mind, Danny gave the trunk an extra stout shove; the car lurched.

He gave the hood an extra resolute push, and just then, looking across, here comes Mr. Oliver Pennick. Danny slapped the hood with both hands; a gesture that he hoped would indicate going somewhere—soon. He lifted his dufflebag and walked to the car. He carried it as if it was an infant in a bassinet. Tenderly, he set it on the passenger seat. The click of the seatbelt, security.

Across the street, Mr. Pennick proceeded resolutely. He passed the mailbox, unexamined, which gave Danny the anxious impression that Mr. Oliver Pennick had been studying all that had been going on and now was on his way here to probe and assess, without any mail checking. Mr. Oliver Pennick tapped his rear pocket perhaps thinking envelopes. He faced Danny head-on, and squinting in his direction, waved.

Danny ducked. He moved to the rear passenger door, creeping low like a movie cowboy crouching behind the boulder before the shooting started. Hunkering, he reached for the handle and opened the door. He stooped over the seat, and while making motions to show he was busy with something, checked on Mr. Oliver Pennick over the dashboard.

Mr. Oliver Pennick stood behind Danny, who, now was drooped over the seat, his legs dangling heavily, butt upward like a duck dabbling at the bottom. Danny could almost feel Mr. Oliver Pennick's stare. He didn't see his smile. Mr. Oliver Pennick came to the open door. Danny didn't see his smile, but he did see him looking through the window at him.

He knocked. "You all right like that?" He stepped back, seemed to take an inventory of the back seat, "You sure got a lot of things back there."

Danny rolled over, sat forward. Legs on the ground. "Hello."

"I see that you're going off somewhere?"

"Yeah. I sure am." Danny opened and closed the door, perhaps to fan Mr. Oliver Pennick away.

"You got everything back there. You going for a long time?"

"Sort of." He stood in front of the dufflebag as a screen.

"Are you going to see your girlfriend?"

"She's not really a girlfriend. Not in that kind of way."

"That's not a good thing. She seemed like she was a real nice gal. Real pretty. If I was you, I'd make her a keeper."

"Yep." He jiggled his keys, loosened the ignition one, and stared over at Mr. Oliver Pennick's mailbox.

"I think I will. In fact I'm getting ready to go to see her now." He wanted to ask him if he'd gotten his mail yet.

"What's her name? Wait, don't say," he pressed Danny's arm, a clutch of narrow fingers, a hand with maroon dots. "Mallorie, right? We had a real nice chat that day."

"Yes. Mallorie." He remembered the day. Mallorie not at all hurried; content to chat with him about everything.

"She told me all about that sewing and stitching she does. Showed me the coat she'd made. She said she forms cloth. Makes it like its plaster or something." Mr. Oliver Pennick pinched his sweater.

"Decoupage. Fabric sculpture," Danny corrected. He closed the door, began to walk away.

Leaning against the door, peering through the window, "What's inside the bag?"

Danny groaned, but Mr. Oliver Pennick did show he'd heard. It'd taken him longer than expected to ask it. He came back to the car.

"Well, Mr. Pennick," he reached for the door, cranked

the window halfway, closed the door. The handle nudged the bag. The contents shifted with a woody rustling, sticks under leafs someone walked on. He opened the door once more, annoyed, then readjusted the bag away from the door and gave it a firm, impatient slam. "I don't know. It's kinda private."

Mr. Pennick moved closer to Danny. He placed a hand on his shoulder. "I'd like to see what you have there. But only if you want to. Only if you're feeling bold."

Danny stepped back half-a pace; Mr. Pennick dropped his hand. They both looked into the window. Danny began, "It's...they're," taking the car keys from his pocket, "they're. It's. Well, you see. That bag," he nodded at it. Now was the time for apologia, for self-conscious regret, to confess his disapproval of self. "They're not really good. They're awful. I can't show them to you." He did indeed care what Mr. Oliver Pennick thought, wanted to explain them. Stop just talking about them. Talked about them, talk, talk, talk, feeling like a wood-a-could-a should have like those guys in the rock band, the ones he'd slapped the tambourine to; the ones without the recording contract they talked about so much.

"You made them. You're proud of them, right?" He made as if to loosen the draw strings himself. "You are what they are; you did your best." He reached out; Danny thought he was going to put his lanky arms around him. "The devil hates a coward."

"They're just heads."

"Heads?"

"Yep. Just heads. Hand carved." Danny sensed the same confusion Mallorie had in Mr. Oliver Pennick's expression. "They're duck heads. Ducks. Just the head."

"Like decoys?" Mr. Pennick, bending close to the window, "For hunting?"

"No hunting. Artwork. Display. They're just the heads." Jabbing the car keys into his palm, wondering where his watch was, wondering if he had the time to explain all of this to Mr. Pennick. "I'm going to take them to a show." He strummed the ignition key across his fingers. A pick on guitar strings.

Mr. Oliver Pennick puzzled his forehead, pressed it against the glass, "Just for show?" His eyeglasses ticked the window. He cupped a hand to look. Danny knew what was coming. "Can I see one?"

"Umm...I kinda got 'me put away. See? I'm just getting ready to leave. I got everything...."

Mr. Pennick didn't hear, "Why that's real interesting, that you make duck heads. I used to hunt with them. Put them out for decoy. When I'd go to the waterways." He looked directly at Danny, "I was a good shot back then." He tapped at the window glass, "So it's just the heads? Mine were all whole. Full-sized ducks." He straightened, adjusted his glasses. "I don't think just heads would do well for hunting."

"No hunting," Danny defended. He stuffed his car keys into another pocket, leaned his elbow against the car door. He scratched at an ear, as if freeing a tick. "They're like sculpture."

Mr. Pennick paused. "Ah. Just to be looked at."

Danny, patient, explanatory, trying, "Well, yeah. Pretty much like that. But more. Me and my...well, you know, Mallorie, we got these plans. Or, more like Mallorie's gotta plan. She's gonna sew. She's got a body. For the duck, I mean. She'll make the bodies. Out of fabric. The chest and arms, wings that is." Danny expanded, waxing artistic, "Like colorful, duck-shaped quilts."

"Stuffed?" Mr. Pennick asked.

"Attached to the heads. She has a soft body ready for the heads."

"You know they won't float. They'll get soaked and sink," Mr. Oliver Pennick said. "Real ducks won't come in."

"I said there're not for hunting."

"Then what do you use them for?"

The conversation was not going the way it was supposed to and Danny wanted to shout, *Jesus-fucking-Christ,*

Mr. Oliv'a-fuck Pennick, they're art objects, but instead he said, "They're going to be for sale. At art shows."

"Craft shows?" Mr. Pennick said, revising it, but not to Danny's satisfaction.

"No. Art shows." Danny let Mr. Pennick ponder that as he pushed a hand into his pants pocket and bunched his car keys. He jiggled them, something to do for a moment, fidgeting while Mr. Pennick rapped at the window. "Ah, well, Mr. Pennick," he took the keys out, "I gotta get to get my..."

Mr. Pennick did not take the fidget hint. "For sale?" He nodded back toward the door. "Can I see one? I just might even buy one." Then, longingly, "I don't have my ducks anymore. Not for years."

He snapped the key chain. "That's too bad."

"Now that I understand that they're not for hunting, can you get one out for looking?"

"No. I mean, yes. You're right; they're not for hunting. But, no, I'm not selling them. Not now."

"I'd say you'd sell me one. I'd say you've done a real fine job making them. From what I've come to learn about you, Daniel Furman, you seem like an awful handy fellow." Stroking his ribs like playing a washboard. "Looks they are a lot of them in there. Seem carefully packed. They must be important to you."

"Thanks. They are." He glanced at the resting duffle bag, snug on the seat, strapped in the belt. Waiting. "But, I gotta get going."

"I'd say there's something in that bag that you're very pleased with."

"I did," Danny said, even proudly; all those previous notions that came and went like the mad menstrual moods women had seemed to swarm like disturbed bees. A buzzing that his work was unsatisfactory, that it was soulfully embarrassing, that all that work was a waste of time, that . "They are." Mr. Pennick's assumptive guess was correct. The duck heads are indeed awful nice. Stunning.

"I'm positive that you've made each one of them," interrupting himself, "you say they're just duck heads?" He waited. "Made them to look awfully wonderful. I can appreciate that you've got a good sense of craftsmanship." He put his arm on Danny's shoulder.

"I do." Now more than ever, inexplicably, assuredly. "I have."

Danny's woodworking success started with failures that began in inadvertently in highschool: Wood Shop. He went into the class flippantly—French was a language for girls. (Of course, years later, sitting around the Sand Pool at Dot Your Eye, he wished he could speak it; now it seemed like an artist's language.) Even though, Wood Shop soon exhibited less than mannish requirements. Danny couldn't help it, but Mr. Letterstock certainly displayed a subtle effeminacy; a *faggot* if Randall had been in the workshop. Mr. Letterstock seemed to have a homoerotic fondness for wood-shaping. Hence, Danny learned two things among the dust and drone of tablesaw and turning lathe: that vocation wasn't gender-specific; and, that it was okay—according to Mr. Letterstock's lively encouragement—to carve shapeless objects.

Well out of highschool, he achieved an uncanny, greater than amateur talent for carving, albeit, recreationally. Soon, the concluding results exhibited striking details that would've made any ornithologist declare admiringly that he did not simply hold a wood replica in hand, but an actual bird; if only just its head.

Well, that's at least what Danny thought, and vainly convinced of it, he continued oblivious to replicate. By experiment and error, Danny learned to fashion his duck heads with knife, carve, and paint so exquisitely that the tufted chin down, the fissured quills, and its tiny neck feathers begged to be stroked.

In large contrast, Danny's timidity and doubted self-confidence defeated him, sending him into a humiliated hollow place. *This stuff is crap, this stuff is crap* a pessimistic voice said, creeping into his self-esteem.

But he was wrong. Over time his whittle bettered.

It did not, of course, come about without the bungle and risk of a novice dabbler. He practiced. He practiced. He indulged. His carving times were often like that of a binge drinker: sporadic, intemperate. It kept him at it for three, sometimes four nights, until feeling so intensely isolated, he'd stop and come off of it exhausted and hungover. And just as a whiskey bender does, there were some stupid accidents, misgivings, and apologetic remorse. He'd used cheap blade-snapping utility knives. He made haphazard purchases; once a discounted carving gouge from which he suffered nick and slice of knuckle.

In his beginnings, there were cross-eyed Mallards, buck-toothed Teals, and tattered Canvasbacks. The neb of his first Redheaded Spoonbill looked as if it was a tongue suppressor, not a beak. The graceful arc of the Duckbill was a crooked spiral. The Merganser's crown, a frying-pan. There were mistakes learned by chance in selecting suitable wood varieties: the slice and splinter of yellow-pine; the tenacious peel of hemlock; the wrest of maple knots; the ruthless grain of oak. At last he found two species he could manage: hickory and ash. Each of these held a stable wood grain, a controlled shave and predictable carve. Both took to brush of paint and wipe of stain with an unvarying acceptance, the result enabling him to present an extraordinary display of artisanship.

Conversely, an equal number of duck-head shapes remain rough-hewn, unfinished, conceptually discarded, and carelessly thrown into the milk crate that was hurriedly packed behind the seat of his car. *Not necessarily mistakes,* Danny rationalized when he'd carried them out of his apartment. *Illusory concepts,* ready to take on ornithological form. That's how Danny defended those that were in-progress.

Although, to be sure, when all was varnished and done, the missing body—the curious absence of a torso—of the unattached head, had a lacking that left the handler wanting to ask, *"Yeah, but? What about?"* Danny would explain that the body was left to the imagination. "The heads are just portraits," he said, "like the busts of Spartans." Leaving it at that; hanging esoterically.

Mr. Oliver Pennick maintained his insistence. "But you did make them to sell, isn't that correct?" He cocked his head, gave Danny an intent look, "You didn't make them just to tote around in that bag, did you?" He cleaned his glasses with a hanky that had appeared as if a magician's. "When a man makes a thing he's proud of, he should show it." Rubbing, "What's the purpose? Not just to hide them." He wadded the hanky, tamped it back in his pocket. "I used collect arrowheads. Still do quite a bit. I've got them laid up in a box at the house. I get them out and show them to folks that say they're interested in them." He stuck his hand into a pocket where another handkerchief was folded. Danny thought Mr. Pennick would blow his nose.

"Like these." He unfolded the cloth bundle as if peeling an orange. Danny watched curiously, setting annoyance away for the moment. "Of course," Mr. Oliver Pennick said modestly, "I didn't make these like you made yours. Indians made these. But, nevertheless, there's a lot of work here." Using his index finger like a jeweler's spatula, he sorted several arrowheads into view, sliding them around the handkerchief as if indeed precious gems. "Would you like to see one," he pinched one between his fingers and held it so that Danny could see.

Danny accepted an arrowhead, struggling to manage impatience, "I don't think...you see, I really gotta go." He took the ignition key from the ring and, using it like a pointer, said, "Like you said, I'm all packed," indicating the jumble in the backseat.

Mr. Oliver Pennick, oblivious, "This one's a deer flint. Razor sharp. A killer. From the Iroquois. Get the feel of it."

Danny took it, fingered the edge, inspected the flint, studied the distinguished scallops, the chiseled hollows, and the primitive, yet precise, workmanship, at its hardness. He felt he knew, could imagine, the sculptor at work. "That's a real nice one," Danny respected thoughtfully. Agreeing more with his self than Mr. Oliver Pennick, "You're right, that's a lot of work." The chiseling was sharp; perhaps even sharper than a few of his carving tools.

"You have got to own sharp instruments, too. Yes?"

Yes, but of course Danny had sharp tools. He'd show some to him if he hadn't stowed them under all that layering in the trunk. Get one out for Mr. Oliver Pennick's assessment. He'd tell Mr. Oliver Pennick how it was that even Randall would concur with sharpness. Although, never as a matter of record, reservedly. Danny was uncertain whether Randall would remember the night, but it was held fast in his memory.

It was an unusually discouraging April evening. By dark-time, some intermittent snowflakes fell wetly. A cloistering chill outside the apartment had lodged Danny and Randall inside unwittingly, like cellmates, not roommates. Randall was in an exceptionally sulky mood. He'd spent his paycheck too early, which kept him impatiently beer-less. Ignoring him, Danny hunkered over his plywood table where he dug, gouged and chipped at an uncooperative piece of wood; snowfall shavings sprinkled as those outdoors did. Randall drifted from the refrigerator door, opening it hopefully and then closed it disappointingly. Then he shuffled over to the window watching nothing, and then sat on the sofa, flipping the pages of his motorcycle magazine with the same attention he'd given through the window. He repeated each of those steps in reverse: off the sofa, to the window, to the fridge; several times, passing behind Danny with an indignant snort. With each pass, Danny was attentive to a riled scent that wafted after Randall. At one point, he stopped in route, stood behind Danny, and reaching around, snatched a curve bladed chisel from the table; the kind that made precise semi-circle incisions easily. He dangled it above Danny, swinging it above Danny's head like the pendulum in the pit from Edgar Allen Poe. "You want to use this right now?" No, of course Danny wasn't using it *right now*, but it was there with the rest of the tools—handy for when he did want to. "I just might want to use this for something myself," Randall mocked, unsettlingly. At first impulse, Danny wanted to seize it out of Randall's hand, but instead, ignored him, letting Randall amuse himself with his dodgy tease; but only briefly. Randall continued his acerbic. "This thing don't seem too sharp." Switching it to his other hand, "Watch, I'll prove it." He pushed it without much firmness or speed into a flat piece of wood. Quickly, the chisel made a neat, surgical, guillotine-like incision through the wood, through the paper underneath it and also further, a quarter-inch into the table under it all, effortlessly. A few half-moon-shaped wood chips fell to the floor, as if curls from a barber's shear. Randall blinked, looked at the fallen whittles stunned. He murmured something. He placed the chisel near Danny, flicked at some of the wood slices with his fingers. "Yeah, I suppose its sharp enough."

Mr. Oliver Pennick had been waiting, watching Danny as he contemplated the arrowhead. "Not nearly as much as the hard work you did in making you sculptures, don't you think?" He arranged some arrowheads. "I'd say your duck heads are just as fine, too. Very real looking." He collapsed the hanky over them. "I'd be hard pressed not to be fully impressed with your handiwork."

His compliments worked. After all, wasn't that the point? Showing and selling. Maybe Mr. Pennick was a discriminating artisan after all. Yes, he was—had been—a shooter of birds, yet, perhaps there might be a naturalist under the shabby, diamond-patterned sweater covering the boney T-shirt. Was there at this last hour here a notion shaping that was empathetic? Yes, he'd known without admitting, that there was a kind man was inside Mr. Pennick—a man who wanted to see his work. For that, he deserved a showing.

Danny unloosened the seatbelt, pulled the dufflebag toward them, and unfastened the bag's grommets. A covey of duck heads stared over the canvas rim as if they were gander awakening from a long wagon ride. Each nestled at ease in an intertwined shred of emerald-plastic grass. Smooth bills, rounded beaks, and flat snouts poked upward; olive-green feathers, jade head, eyes like black beans on a salad. Iridescent eyes beseeched an equal exchange.

Mr. Pennick leaned in, he almost resting on Danny's shoulder. "Goodness," he exclaimed, "I didn't think that Loringer's still made that grass stuff." He squeezed it and with that same squeezing he pushed his hand into the bag, ready to reach for a duckhead. "You've got a lot of them in there."

Danny bolted. "Here, I'll get it for you," taking Mr. Pennick's mottled wrist and drawing it away. Danny took one out and as if handing Mr. Pennick a freshly baked roll, put it in his hand.

"Gosh, son, they surely are gorgeous. Realistic, too." Appreciating, Mr. Pennick held it between both palms.

Danny nodded, folded his arms across his chest, pleased with Mr. Oliver Pennick's delight. Danny gave him another one.

"Oh, look indeed. A Bufflehead!" And then another. "And jeepers, a Canvasback." He petted it. "My favorite."

And Danny's also. Its stately forehead, long graceful neck, distinguishing cinnamon collar, and prideful posture made it look like a duck who knew the benefits of peaceful floating. More importantly, a canvasback represented Mallorie—her straightforward eyes, the wide crown of her forehead, her secret demure smile. Knowing. "Yes, sir. Mine too." Danny said, sir, newly respectful of Mr. Oliver Pennick. He rubbed its bill, as if he shared unknowingly Danny's admiration for Mallorie.

Danny brought out a few more. He set them on the trunk hood. Clearly, Danny reflected, Mr. Pennick knew his duck species. Danny presumed that Mr. Pennick had a devout reverence for them; even as they lay dead from gunshot.

Danny produced two canvasbacks. A mallard, a coot, and yet another bufflehead. Danny especially liked them, the buffleheads with their perfectly round, cartoon-like roundness with its convex curve and its stubby beak, making them seem as if they should have nicknames like Huey, Dewey, or Louie—the Walt Disney darlings.

Still in the duffle remained wood ducks, the ones with the downward bill and the tiny hook at the tip so that if it could speak, it would be with a lisp. And marsh dabbers, with their defining paddle bill, doing just that, dabbing. He had hooded mergansers, sleek-backed, winged crowns that if seen on a pond could look like a nun in a habit, shoulder deep in the water. He'd carved some coots. An oddly turned bill, embarrassed expression, an unflattering name accomplished the perfect comedy.

"These are real prizes, son. I'll bet you've had them for long time." He patted two of the heads.

"Years. I've been all over the place with these things."

"And I'd say that you're going to take them over to that new gal-friend of yours too, aren't you?" He winked.

"Yes, sir." He stood while Mr. Oliver Pennick examined each one, as if nesting a fallen bird. He complimented Danny on each hand-sculpted detail with the point of a skeletal finger and stroke of freckly hand. "Gosh," he whispered, "such tiny feathers. And would you look at the beautiful colors on this Teal."

Danny did not have to. He'd used a special lacquer. It gave the teal's multicolored scalp a remarkably natural sheen, bringing out its iridescence, as if naturally. Recalling the process, he smelled the volatile fumes and that aroma memory took him back quickly to the very night—in fact, Danny could almost see the hands on the clock above the kitchen stove—that he'd labored with tiny brush and pointy knife as he painted and chiseled the teal into life— the convincing features as if it were actually alive and had just emerged from its shallow-water feeding, wet and glistening.

"You know, the teal only feeds just below the water surface," Mr. Pennick announced as if suddenly recalling it. "They're kind just dabbles and dips." He bobbed his head mimicking the duck feeding.

Danny was overwhelmed. Not in a startled, shocked manner, but in a sort of profound way. He stared closer at the old man, the wizened cheeks, the barely noticeable but graying bearded stubble, the thick eyebrow bush, and now difficult to say a compliment, the lustrous false teeth. He noticed anew Mr. Pennick's ears, like well-worn catcher's mitts. The black hairs like the quills of a whistle duck. How the circlet on his temple resembled that of a Stiftail.

Eventually, Mr. Pennick said, "I should be home. You have to go somewhere. I can tell that you need to go to there."

"That's right. Okay." Danny gathered his ducks. He nestled them into the Easter grass shavings deep inside his dufflebag as if storing heirloom Christmas ornaments in straw. He withheld the last one, the elegant Canvasback. He held it reverently, knowing Mr. Oliver Pennick was watching. "Wait." He lifted his ancient speckled hand, unwrapped the spindly fingers, and placed the Canvasback in the center of them. "Here, Mr. Oliver Pennick. You can have this one." With both palms, he held it dearly, as if a communion wafer.

He didn't stammer, but nearly. "Why, thank you very, very much." Finishing that, he did stammer. "I like this one real," he paused, and Danny though for a fleeting moment that a handkerchief would come up. "I mean, it's so special." Mr. Pennick stroked the distinctively descending combs that are the Canvasback's pleats. "I'll consider it good luck from a very special neighbor."

"I know. I mean, you're welcome." He closed the bag, cinched its draw stings, pushed it upright, pulled the seatbelt round, and closed the door.

Mr. Pennick turned, wobbled toward the driveway, and then stopped. He dug into his pocket. He pulled out his folded up handkerchief. He took an arrowhead—the long and narrow one with the cupped serrations that Danny had admired—and went back to him and put it into his hand, just as Danny had done for him. He tapped it lightly saying, "Here, for you Daniel Furman, my friend. To your good future."

They stood mutely for a few moments, each admiring each treasure. Danny pinched the arrowhead's diamonded shaft between his fingers like he'd found a doubloon — those same wire pinching, pliers-like fingers that just a couple of hours ago had fixed the radio. The scalloped flares at the edge of the flint were like the raked-back scoop of an Elder duck's fletching.

Mr. Oliver Pennick nodded, suggesting the flint in Danny's hand, "It's a real old one, just like me." He grinned graciously. Synthetic, newly white teeth beamed from their pinkly opaque gums.

"You're not old," surprised that he'd said it.

"How old do you suppose I am?"

He didn't want to guess. He didn't have the time. Did he have to remind again that he was trying to leave; go to where Mallorie was? Even though, he guessed lightheartedly. He held the flint up. "Not as old as this?"

The allegory was misplaced. Unexpectedly, Mr. Oliver Pennick brooded. "I'm in a place here," he cast a pensive glance at his house and shrugged at something up the street that signaled to Danny that *here* wasn't any of those places, "where I've lived longer in the past than I suspect that I'll now live in the future."

This is awkward Danny struggled.

As if sensing it, "That's okay." Pointing at the arrowhead, "No, not that old," changing leg-standing, "I've had a long life so far. There are some who don't have a good long life."

Again, Danny struggled. He had nowhere to go with someone not having a good long life. Again he showed the arrowhead, sympathetically. "So, I've got good fortune now," inquiring about it unsurely. Danny grinned as Mr.

Oliver Pennick had a moment ago, but not at all like the wide grin that had smiled across from him.

"You are welcome, Daniel." He turned away, looked out the driveway, came back. "By the way, where's that galfriend of yours now?"

"She's there waiting for me."

Mr. Oliver Pennick made his way across the checkerboarded street. His left shoe shuffled, whooshed, and his right shoe shuffled, swooshed all the way passed his mailbox. At the curb, Mr. Pennick called out, "You be careful now. Rest well." He moved his stilt-like legs over the curb, and up the steps to his front porch where he stood, waved and shouted—more like the call of a raspy yodeler than a shout—"And please give that sweet honey gal of yours a big hug when see her. Where ever she is now."

"Will do." Where Mallorie was now, that place where she would be, materialized as a dazzling image, as if her absolute presence had just walked out from the photograph of her.

Danny stood on an empty driveway, next to a fully packed car, finally. At last. Done. Danny took a one last glimpse at the apartment door—the gouged wood—and shook his head as if the door-splitting memory would shake out. He slid behind the steering wheel. He slipped the key into the ignition. He turned the radio on. A disquieting noise. He turned it off. Now he liked silence; it allowed him to recall Mr. Pennick's naively directed questions, that at first seemed rude and probing, but now how utterly harmless they were. Had been.

And all of those other questions; how irrelevant they are now: *Where do you get it? What do you make them for? How come? What's back there in that bag? You do? Is it sharp? They're just heads? Why? What are you going to do with them? Where's that gal-friend of yours now?"*

Really? Danny didn't know. "Because I can," he said aloud, and not to himself, but to someone else—Mallorie.

Danny pulled the key from the ignition. He paused, contemplating the appearance of a shrouded figure next to him. There between him and his dufflebag was a whitish silhouette, a sheet-covered contour over wing-shaped points, a pale shadow configured as a palm. He raised the sheet in the way a magician reveals his surprise. There is was, the curling W of wing-like boughs, the open fronds, the vanes of a fan enveloping the hidden things inside them—Mallorie's sculpture. His sculpture. The—*hands?* The *wings?* Beckoning.

But wait. Wait until he tells her all about it. Tells her what Mr. Pennick said. Shows her the arrowhead. She'll giggle at it. *Ouch, it's sharp!* At all of it. The frivolous rhetoric. Then she'll sweep her hair over her shoulders, poke his ribs, and she'll say something like, *I didn't know what time you'd get here; it doesn't matter* Then Danny will bring in her cloth statuettes, her sculpture. Safely delivered. He'll hold them out for her to see. *I'm glad you came.* He'll watch her smile spread like sculptured fronds. Her face, softly pale will glimmer brightly in its whiteness. She'll ask if he brought his duckheads. *Are they here?* Yes, they're right over there. Her eyes will shine bright, boundless and multicolored. Of these things, Danny does know.

Daniel Furman. He sat upright. He adjusted the incline comfortably. His head relaxed against headrest. His arm, the one he can wave, is stretched, ready to change the rearview mirror; the crack in it splits the image behind him. His other arm, the one he can wrap around Mallorie's sculpture embraces it, holds it to him, securely, safely...eternally.

The Devil Hates a Coward

Heart Knots

You see the way it was, was that bad time me and Kiley had at the bus place. That's when she told me that I should'a looked at it someplace else because she couldn't show me then. She made it like if I really wanted to see it, and really wanted to know what it's like and get it the decent way, then I should just look it up like someplace better. I didn't say anything then. But I thought I could've said it, but still didn't then. Kiley just turned away to the other girls. Plus which, and she said this to the other girls, that even if I did, I'd probably be too stupid to understand it. The other girls kinda nodded like I was. Kiley said it was a fiddly thing. She'd never said fiddly before. But she says words like that when she's trying to act bigger, like as if she's an after school girl and things and she didn't have to get on the bus like I was. I don't know what's fiddly, but she made it out in a more meaner way than like how I'm saying. But, I can tell you she said I was stupid. And you know what? Right after that she even kicked my shoe and called me a louse. A stupid louse.

And then hollered loud so's those others could hear,

Go look it up, you stupid louse, and poked her face and looked at me cross-eyed saying, like in your Aunty Pikey's dictionary. She said that about Aunt Pikey in a nasty way, like as if then she didn't even care for Aunt Pikey. But that's not always. There's other times she cares about Aunt Pikey, even though she's my aunt and not hers. But I guess not so much when she was mad like that and was telling me what to do. I think you know my Aunt Pikey likes Kiley. She says Kiley's a peach. Says it like when Kiley's right there with me and winks when she says it. More like squeezing her eyes than winking the way old ladies do when they're trying to make it like you're together on something.

Even after Kiley kicked my shoe and was staring at me I didn't say anything. She said there might even be some kind of a picture with it. Then, she told those other girls that I couldn't use the computer. You know I can use it; it's just that my dad says it's better if I use the dictionary. Or the encyclopedia. Then Kiley said there probably wouldn't be one anyways because it'd be real hard to show such a thing. Finally I said something and told her if there was, I'd draw it or copy it down or something and show her how I got it. Must've been something like in the way I said it because she kicked me again. At my leg. But I didn't make like it hurt and that seemed like it made her madder and she slapped my books down and got on her bus. Mad like.

When I was on my bus and no one was seeing, I rubbed my leg. That was Friday. We haven't talked since then. It's not like I can't. We do sometimes. She's got her own phone, but she lives way over by Breezewood. And anyways, I'm not allowed riding my bike over there.

So the next day I did what she wanted and looked for it in the dictionary. Not the little paper one that mom gave me. That one's at school. I mean the big one. The one that Aunt Pikey gave us for Christmas some time ago. It's got its own table, but you have to keep a cardboard piece under the leg because it wobbles. So you gotta be careful opening pages or it gets tippy. My dad always says to keep it opened to the M pages. He says it has to be that way because it's better for it to be spread open even that way in the middle pages. I suppose it's so the edging doesn't stretch if it's more to another letter, like S or C. So I always keep it open that way so it stays the way he says. That's okay. Besides, that way no one'll know the words I'd been looking at after when I'd opened it. One time I saw it where it was left at the word mammary and switched the pages so that mom didn't think it was me that where I was looking. So I turned some pages away and checked it and then it was showing menstrual and then that've been worser because when I saw that it might seem I like I was looking at it on purpose. I think my mom might be worried about what I was doing looking at that word even though I did. So I turned some pages again and it was Mars and that'd be okay because she knows I like Martians.

My dad says it's okay for me to look up words. He's got lots of dictionaries on his shelves. Some have nothing but charts in them. One's got Latin. There's this one with the parts of a house like the ones we have but its got nothing but sheer drawings. He thinks I should know them. The dictionary words that is. Not big words but regular words like in the big dictionary on the table. I would never tell him I looked at menstrual. One time we looked up deciduous for when I had my leaf collection for school. I saw that deer antlers are deciduous too. Some words after that was decimate, and dad laughed at that was a good word, saying that's how I ate my cereal. He said I should know other words and not always fully in their meaning but how I could make sense of them in sentences later. He says that a real book is better than the computer.

Actually, I really do like looking stuff up in books. And you know just because Kiley had told me to, doesn't make it that it's the only ways I do. There's been sometimes that me and Kiley look at things together. And not even just because it's for homework. I don't always just look at

Heart Knot

words so much but at the pictures next to them too. Well, they're not really pictures like regular pictures. They're like drawings somebody's made. Real tiny ones made like with a pencil or a little bitty pen or something. But they're drawn real good. Not like I could. Those dictionary pictures aren't like the ones in the encyclopedia. Those are all colored and shiny and more bigger. The dictionary one's are black and small and are on just a part of the page.

Except for knots. At knots there's almost a whole page of them drawn real nice. There's all kinds of knots that are tied around sticks and posts and metal hooks and stuff. Some are plain and not tied around things. They're just hoops open in the air with nothing inside them like you're supposed to pretend that the knot could be tied around something else. The ropes aren't smooth ropes like clothesline rope is. They're more like boat ropes. Kinda furry and scratchy looking. My favorite's the prolung or prolow or I guess something like that. Anyways, it's complicated. At first it looks like it's got two ropes tied around each other into a bigger knot, but if you look closer at it and trace it together, it's really all just one rope tied into two knots joined at once. Hard to figure out until you see it. That knot—I'll say it's called the prolow—is one of the knots that's not tied around anything. No post or nothing to hold it. So when you see it, you'd see how it's just two round hoops curled around nothing except each other. I tried making it like that, like I was a sailor, but I had to use a smooth rope from the laundry room. After awhile I got it and it looked pretty much like the picture.

Then I looked up sailboat and there were some pictures of some but not as many as knots, but near the boats there was a picture of a sailfish. You know, it's like a swordfish except with a tinier mouth. They both got pointed mouths so they can stab their food.

One time I looked up penis but there wasn't a picture of a penis. Just words. Course Kiley wasn't there then. There wasn't a picture of a vagina there either. Just words. They don't say much, but I remember them. They said about it being a passage leading to the vulva in female mammals. That's all I wanna say now. It's kinda embarrassed how I remember the words in that way. One time I wanted to look up vagina in the encyclopedias, but they're up in my sister's room and she doesn't even have them all. Some of the letter books are gone. I think K and maybe S, which is too bad because did you know most words start with S? Besides, she's in her room all the time and I don't go in there when she is. Especially not to look up vagina. So I looked it up in the school library and you know there was a picture of one but it was just all by itself and it didn't even have the whole girl with it. It was an older girl be-

Heart Knot

cause there were hairs on it. Not like my sister. I pretended to be looking up viaduct instead of vagina but kept my finger at viaduct just in case. Viaduct would be okay to look at if someone'd seen.

Anyways, as I was saying, I went to Aunt Pikey's dictionary and when I went to look up the word Kiley said I was supposed to, I saw it was still the same page that I'd left it opened to. The one I wanted seen opened. There was still the picture of the mongoose there. I like the mongoose. All I can say to you it's sorta like a weasel or a mink or a stretched out rat and on the picture of it it's got a mean grin and little sharp teeth in its mouth. The mongoose lives in Asia. They eat mice and birds and large beetles and stuff like that. I think they can kill snakes too. But I wanted to do what Kiley had told me. So I opened the pages to L.

To look up love.

It's funny because louse is on the same page. And even more funnier then was that louse is right above louver. Just like the ones at my school's window. I got a pencil and paper. I figured maybe after I'd found the word, I'd write Kiley a note from the words by it. Sorta like a poem letter. I felt like drawing a picture with it and get some words under love that'd be good sounding words. Big words, like when we used to look at the dictionary together and Kiley said those bigger words. One time it was carcinoma. That time she wrote the words down mainly to herself and then kept them inside her pocket and didn't tell me why.

So like Kiley had, I wrote down the words to myself. I picked special words and made them into curvy lines like they were ropes and made them look tied together for my picture to her. I got a nice little box and took the rope poem up to my bedroom and put it inside the box. Then I thought of another idea. Away back, I found this glass heart. It's mostly pink, but not pink like pretty pink. More like crystal pink. It's just like a marble but shaped in a heart and real smooth and you can see into it and see all the different colors that are inside it just like a real marble except that it's not a round marble. I got some nice colored pieces out of my mom's crochet things and I tied that knot I'd been telling you about, the prolunge or something, and tied the two knots together real carefully around the heart and made it like it was in a nest or something and put it in the box with my note poem.

On Sunday night, before school, I checked it all and the knot seemed like it was all still good. And see that I still liked the rope poem so I put them away until the next day.

Anyways, like I was saying about what happened with Kiley and me at the bus place. You see the way it was, was about what I didn't tell you. She wanted me to say I love

Heart Knot

her. Like, say to her, I love you. I didn't say it. Well, not like I wouldn't but more so I couldn't. I'd thought I'd had, that is, said it in kinda of a way before then. But I guess not in the way she wanted me to say it. And it's even kinda hard for me to say it to you like this in this way now. You not being Kiley and all, you know. Well, not like saying it to you in the way for Kiley. You know what I mean? Saying it other ways, not like in the way I'm telling you now. Maybe that's what a fiddly thing is.

So then when Monday came, I went to school and all day I had the box. Then, when we were outside I gave her the box. She looked at it happy and opened it and read the rope poem—and even touched the words—and felt the knot I'd tied around the heart and then she hugged me a whole bunch and I thought she was going to kiss me but she didn't and then she looked at it more happy again and said they were beautiful words. That's when she asked me to tell her that I love her. Again. Like on last Friday. Say I love you she said. I didn't say anything. I mean I didn't say I love her. I don't know why? I just didn't say anything. I showed her how I made the things inside the box and how the rope poem was and how I'd tied the prolow knot around the glass marble heart and sorta guessed that all those things would be the way I did. But she just kept looking at me when I was showing and when I stopped and said nothing about loving her, all of the sudden she got real mad and threw down the heart, real hard, and walked away. And then she hollered, but not facing me but facing upwards away, that I was a stupid louse. Like all over again.

About the Author

Peter Hamilton writes "Interrogative Fiction". He is a columnist for newspapers and magazines. A member of The Authors' Guild; Associated Writers' and Publishers'; Chautauqua Literary and Scientific Circle; The Gotham Writers' Group and other affiliates, his work has been accepted at Vermont College of Fine Arts, Sewanee Writers Conference; StoneCoast; and Alkonkian Retreat. He is the organizational facilitator for the annual Vineyard Writers' Conference. He lives in Sherman, NY.

Made in the USA
Charleston, SC
08 March 2015